SUNFLOWERS

Incredible Journeys of Epic Women Artists from India

Sujata Parashar

ATLANTIC
PUBLISHERS & DISTRIBUTORS (P) LTD

ATLANTIC
PUBLISHERS & DISTRIBUTORS (P) LTD
7/22, Ansari Road, Darya Ganj, New Delhi
Tel.: +91-11-4077 5252, 2327 3880
E-mail: orders@atlanticbooks.com
Web: www.atlanticbooks.com

Published by Atlantic Publishers & Distributors (P) Ltd 2024

Photo Credits: Arindam Sen

Disclaimer

- The author and the publisher have taken every effort to the maximum of their skill, expertise and knowledge to provide correct material in the book. Even then if some mistakes persist in the content of the book, the publisher does not take responsibility for the same. The publisher shall have no liability to any person or entity with respect to any loss or damage caused, or alleged to have been caused directly or indirectly, by the information contained in this book.
- The author has fully tried to follow the copyright law. However, if any work is found to be similar, it is unintentional and the same should not be used as defamatory or to file legal suit against the author.
- If the readers find any mistakes, we shall be grateful to them for pointing out those to us so that these can be corrected in the next edition.
- All disputes are subject to the jurisdiction of Delhi courts only.

Printed & bound in India by Atlantic Print Services

A Tribute to Indian Women in Art

Advance Praise

"Live the dilemma, go through the indecisiveness. Through it all, you will find something. Latch on to it. Don't run away from its fire because what is manifesting as fire will burn away all the dirt, all the rubbish, and pure art will remain—priceless, immeasurable, something that can never be taken away from you.

Sujata Parashar cuts through the lives of young women artists and slices them smoothly to serve extraordinary life stories of women, whose destiny chose to be artists. A must read."

Prathibha Prahlad

Padmasree & Sangeet Natak Akademi Awardee
Founder & Managing Trustee,
Prasiddha Foundation & Forum For Art Beyond Borders
Founder Festival Director, Delhi International Arts Festival

"कलाकार औरतें सूफ़ी कवियों के रहस्यवाद की तरह होती हैं। ऐसा लगता है कि वो समझ आ रही हैं लेकिन नहीं आतीं। ऐसा लगता है कि 'घूँघट के पट' खुल रहे हैं लेकिन पूरी तरह नहीं खुलते। वैसे उनका समझ आना ज़रूरी नहीं है, ज़रूरी है उन्हें समझने की कोशिश करना। कोशिश से बेहतर किसी भी भाषा में कोई भी शब्द ईजाद नहीं हुआ। क्योंकि ईमानदार कोशिश हमेशा रोचक होती है। जैसे यह किताब- जो कोशिश भी है, ईमानदार भी और रोचक भी।"

(Women artists are just like mystic Sufi poets. You think you understand them but you don't. You feel the veil is being removed but it's not lifted completely. It's not necessary to understand them but it's important to make an effort to do so. There's no better word in a language than effort because honest attempts are thrilling just like this book which is not only an honest attempt but also a thrilling one.)

इरशाद कामिल

बॉलीवुड गीतकार और कवि
(Irshad Kamil, Bollywood lyricist and Poet)

"सुजाता पाराशर ने अपनी नई किताब में बदलते भारत की 12 महिलाओं से परिचय कराया है। यह पुस्तक कुछ सिर्फ महिलाओं की लाइफ जर्नी नहीं है, हमारे दौर में अलग-अलग तरीके से समय से जूझ रही महिलाओं का परिचय है। जिसमें पुणे (महाराष्ट्र) से हिना सिद्दीकी हैं, मधुबनी (बिहार) से श्वेता झा, पंजाब से Kanika ढिल्लन तो असम से शिल्पा बारदलोई आदि। देश के अलग-अलग हिस्से की ये महिलाएं भारतीय समाज में औरत का बदलता चेहरा दिखाती हैं, जो अपनी स्वतंत्र पहचान से एक नई इबारत लिख रही है।"

(In her new book, Sujata Parashar has introduced us to twelve women of changing India. This book isn't only about the life journeys of a few women but it's a depiction of women of this era and the different ways they're dealing with life-challenges. We get a glimpse of women representing different parts of the country, like, Hina Siddiqui from Pune, (Maharashtra), Sweta Jha from Madhubani (Bihar), Kanika Dhillon from Amritsar (Punjab) and Shilpa Bordoloi from Jorhat (Assam) and many more. Their stories show us the changing face of women in today's society. Through their independent identities they're expressing themselves anew.)

प्रताप सोमवंशी

मैनेजिंग एडीटर, हिन्दुस्तान, हिन्दी डेली

(Pratap Somvanshi, Managing Editor, Hindustan, Hindi Daily)

"Sujata Prashar's 'Sunflowers' is a rare bouquet of biographical stories of women artists, which are at once deeply moving and inspiring. Her honest approach makes us meet the artists almost 'in person', as they relive their personal and creative journeys. The compelling narratives of the Theatre artists Hina Sidiqui and Shilpika Bordoloi map the personal course their lives take against the geographic, social and economic backdrops—a must read by the artists and the others."

Ramanjit Kaur,

Founder Director,
The Creative Arts, National Vice-President,
Arts Leadership Council, Women Indian Chamber of Commerce and Industry

In 'Sunflowers', gifted novelist and poet Sujata Parashar explores the rich mosaic of feminine creativity. Delving into the life stories, artistic contributions, and influences of women artists from various domains, Sujata offers a compelling perspective of their inspirations and the significance of their art. 'Sunflowers' is an essential read for anyone who wants to understand the profound role female artists play in nurturing the soul of society.

Vinita Dawra Nangia
Executive Editor,
Times Group

Foreword

Art is one of the creative form of expression and a powerful medium to enhance varied ways of thinking and looking at things. There's no denying that in today's world, art is more important than ever to face new situations and challenges in life. India is known for its rich art and culture around the world. In fact, from the very beginning, art has been influencing all areas of life in Indian society, whether it's cultural, religious or even social activities. Could we value our art and heritage more? Could we find more meaning in it and from it?

As the world moves to artificial intelligence, we ask: what will drive the new big ideas? Creators, Makers, Ideators, Artists, and more. For a long time in India, a career in the arts was not promoted, in fact we have severely ignored our heritage but today, things are changing. Artists are storytellers, and we are giving them their due. No science, no math and no idea is complete without a story.

Sujata's collection of short biographies of twelve exceptional Indian women artists representing different fields of art is an attempt to address and change this mindset. Through the powerful real-life stories of the featured female artists, Sujata has tried to show how, if inculcated at a young age and pursued with passion and dedication (and encouragement), art not only enriches the artist but also contributes to the economic and social well-being of a nation. This book is not about art but about the artists as individuals, believers, leaders and pathbreakers. It sews together what shaped their thinking and turned them into the accomplished individuals they are today despite facing various challenges. The book also highlights how the artists have excelled at their artistic endeavours, made it financially viable but also celebrated art as a profession that impacts and inspires.

The engaging stories in the book are replete with anecdotal experiences of the featured artists as told to the author by the twelve contributors, including their family, friends and associates, respectively. I'm sure this book will inspire the country's youth to not only engage with the different forms of art but also pursue them as a profession. My best wishes!

Shaili Chopra
Founder, SheThePeopleTV, Author and Journalist

Preface

I imagine, therefore I create.

Dear Readers,

I'm an accidental writer.

I started writing only in my early thirties. Before that, I'd led the life of a (professional) gipsy, playing different roles in contrasting fields. From working for an international airline to spearheading exciting projects in the social development sector and even a short stint as a startup entrepreneur in Singapore, I gathered a rich and diverse experience in different professions. Yet, it was only when I started writing that I knew I had finally found my calling.

The success of my first novel catapulted me into the world of writing, and also helped me discover a different side of my personality. However, I realised I had to prove to myself and those around me that the book wasn't just a fluke. I felt like I truly had it in me, so I wrote another novel, and that's how my writing journey began.

Today, after writing 12 books, I feel happy that I listened to (and acted on) my calling after my first attempt. May be it was luck, or may be it was perseverance. There were many hurdles in my path that could have easily swayed me. From my own doubts and apprehensions regarding my writing ability, to my broken marriage and a young child whom I'd to practically raise on my own, my financial worries and so many other factors that I can't put into words here troubled me for a long time. However, I overcame them and continued writing, and I'm thankful I managed it all well.

That brings me to this particular book.

I've often wondered about artists and the kind of people they must have been before they realised their potential and started walking the artistic path. Did they always know they would choose this path? What was their motivation? After all, it's not easy to be an artist in a country like India where we as a collective take pride in our art and culture, but as individuals (and as parents), we think of it like a side dish: to be enjoyed but not as something that can foster our personal and material growth.

The twelve female artists featured in this book represent different fields of art. Each is an exceptional artist and has made a name for herself. It is even more remarkable that they didn't simply stop there; their work and individual effort in positively impacting people and the planet show how artists can meaningfully contribute to society.

This book is not only an attempt to understand the heart and mind of an artist (specifically those who are female), including showcasing their challenges and achievements, but it also highlights the power of art and how it can successfully achieve a change in mindsets and break old biases without having to resort to force or diplomacy.

Some may wonder why I focused only on female artists for this book. The reason is simple: I wanted to explore how challenging it might be for a woman to become an artist in a patriarchal setting like ours. Is there a price they pay for their success? How did these women cope with the different challenges that came their way? Their success stories also show the dreams and aspirations of the new age Indian woman and how she's enthusiastically claiming her space.

I hope the incredible stories of the featured artists in this book give you a good glimpse of what goes into the making of an artist. I also hope it encourages you to appreciate artists as creative nurturers of society.

Keep Smiling!

Sujata Parashar

June 2022, Delhi

Acknowledgements

First, I would like to thank my parents for their unwavering love and support in all my pursuits, followed by my son, Lokevidu. He was perhaps the most overlooked in this process due to my frequent travelling and being glued to laptop to finish writing this book. By the time I finished writing this book, Vidu was already in Vancouver, starting his new (college) life. I miss him.

I would also like to extend my gratitude to the WICCI Delhi Arts Council for supporting the official launch of the book in Delhi. A special mention and heartfelt thanks to Beena Unnikrishnan, National President, WICCI Arts Council; Ramanjeet Kaur, Vice President, WICCI Arts Council; Ishani Chandra, President, WICCI Delhi Arts Council; Harpreet Kaur Jass; Member, WICCI Delhi Arts Council; and Nalini Malviya, President, Bangalore WICCI Arts Council for helping me identify some of the prodigious female artists featured in the book. Ishani and Harpreet were especially generous, acting as sounding boards for the project.

My heartfelt thanks also to my writer-friends Shinie Antony and Prateek Sur, as well as well-known theatre professional Mahrukh Barucha, for helping me with the name list. I must also thank my dear friend and fellow author, Shabri Prasad for supporting me in this journey. A shout out to my good friend Arindam Sen for helping me out with the photos and the videos.

My deepest gratitude to Bharatnatyam Dancer and Padmashree awardee Pratibha Prahlad ji for the beautiful blurb; Shaili Chopra, Founder, SheThePeople network for the book's lovely foreword. I'm also indebted to Shri Irshad Kamil, Bollywood lyricist and Poet; Vinita Dawra Nangia, Executive Editor Times Group (Entertainment and Style); Pratap Somvanshi, Managing Editor, Hindustan Hindi Daily; Ramanjit Kaur, Founder Director, The Creative Arts and National VP, WICCI Arts Leadership Council for their generous appreciation.

This is an offbeat book for someone like me who primarily writes fiction. The thought of finding a suitable publisher for the book did give me a niggling of doubt, but thankfully, I had the solid backing of my literary agency, The Book Bakers. Suhail Mathur and team, thank you for believing in me and my idea and pitching the book to the right publisher.

My deepest gratitude to Atlantic Publishers for taking up this book. Because of them, the incredible stories of these artists will see the light of day and (hopefully) encourage and inspire young people to engage with art in a deeper way. I must make a special mention of my editors, Namarita Kathait and her team at Atlantic, and Sneha Baweri for the care and precision given to the book to make it a pleasurable read.

The brilliant female artists featured in this book deserve a standing ovation for not only agreeing to share their stories, but also for enduring my hundreds of questions. Thank you from the bottom of my heart. Also, many thanks to the families, friends, teachers, colleagues, and associates of all the artists for enriching the book with their insights. Lastly, my gratitude to the universe for guiding me and giving me the confidence to complete this huge project.

Introduction

India is a country of many paradoxes. Our diversity is our strength and makes us one of the most unique cultures in the world. However, when we speak of the great contrasts of our nation, one of the most straightforward examples is the way artists across the board are received by our society. On one hand, Indians are proud of their culture and creativity. It reflects in every area of their socio-cultural life. However, on the other hand, the reality is that artists have often been neglected and not given the respect and support they deserve. Artists are excluded from mainstream social and political discussions. Studies across the world have impressed upon the importance of art education. Experts and thought leaders have exalted the power of the arts in moving people's hearts and helping them find peaceful ways of engaging and solving conflicting socio-economic issues of the world. Yet, in our own country, where a vast range of creativity is reflected through its arts, it's given a low priority.

This book is an attempt to address this issue by portraying the real-life stories of some exceptional young women artists of the country. It talks about their childhood, their dreams and aspirations in their youth, the hurdles they faced, their achievements and how they're impacting people and the planet through their work. This book also aims to study the cultivation of the artistic mind, including the impact of the external environment on the artist, and further hopes to inspire the youth to pursue art not only as a viable career but also as a creative tool to bring positive change.

The title, "Sunflowers", was carefully chosen to show the qualities of an artist and how—like a sunflower—they're not only beautiful, vibrant and resilient but also have the power to put forth creative solutions to the world's problems with their art. The individual stories of the featured artists are divided into three different parts, named according to the different stages of growth of a sunflower:

Star Bud (Childhood)

The first part is dedicated to the artists' childhood experiences, memorable events, and the views of close family members, including their siblings, friends and teachers, to give an idea to the readers about the environment they grew up in that helped them develop and nurture their talent.

Ray Floret (Youth)

This segment will focus on the period before the artists established themselves and became popular in their respective fields. It deals with the trials and tribulations they experienced before their first break.

Full Bloom (Name and Fame)

In this section, the featured artists talk about their present life—their accomplishments, the story behind the success of their projects, and how their art has influenced or impacted modern Indian society. This part will also shed light on the artists' future projects, goals, and dreams.

The aim of art is to spread joy, peace and new ways of thinking. Moreover, through their work, artists present creative and thoughtful ways of resolving conflicts. I hope the stories of the twelve creative contributors in this book reflect this idea effectively and clearly and inspire the readers to recognise, appreciate and engage with art closer than ever.

Contents

1
Arushi Mudgal

Odissi Dancer

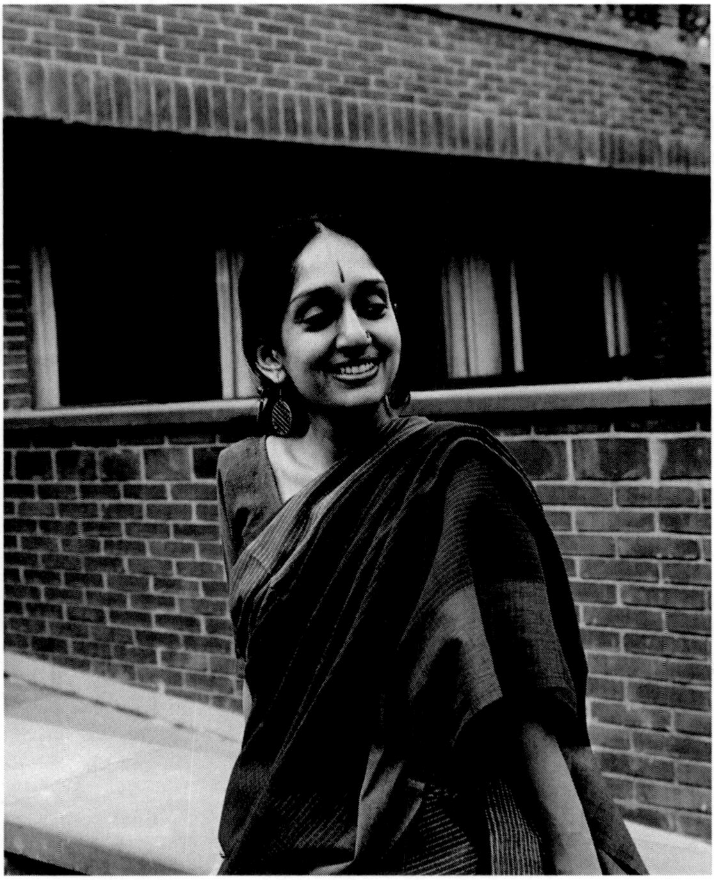

Figure 1

"Your relationship with art has to be honest."

—Arushi Mudgal

ARUSHI MUDGAL (b. 1986) is one of the foremost talents in the field of *Odissi*. She was trained under her aunt, Madhavi Mudgal, an internationally acclaimed Odissi dancer known for her unique contribution to the evolution of the classical dance form. Madhavi*ji* taught Arushi at the Gandharva Mahavidyalaya, Delhi. This premiere music and dance institution was founded by Arushi's grandfather Pt. Vinaya Chandra Maudgalya, and currently her father Pt. Madhup Mudgal an accomplished Hindustani Classical Vocalist heads it.

Arushi has been featured in several prestigious platforms in the country: the Music Academy, Krishna Gana Sabha, Karthik Fine Arts, Brahma Gana Sabha (Chennai), the Nishagandhi Festival (Trivandrum), NCPA, NMACC (Mumbai), and Sangeet Natak Akademi's Yuva Puraskar Festival (Delhi), among several others. She has also performed extensively at various art festivals in the USA, UK, France, Brazil, Austria, Germany, Spain, Belgium, Greece, China, Malaysia and Singapore. In 2018, The New York Times selected her as one of the Top Ten Dancers. Alastair Macaulay, the Chief Dance Critic of the New York Times, wrote, "I was amazed by how fully she seemed one of India's most remarkable dancers".

She is a recipient of the Ustad Bismillah Khan Yuva Puraskar, a national award given by the Central Sangeet Natak Akademi. She has also had the privilege of performing for dignitaries like former Indian President Shri Abdul Kalam, former President Shri Pranab Mukherjee, Prime Minister Shri Narendra Modi, and former President of USA, Mr. Barack Obama, at the Rashtrapati Bhavan, New Delhi.

There's no denying that Arushi has acquired enormous fame and success at a very young age. She's one of the most accomplished young *Odissi* dancers in the country. Born and brought up in a distinguished family of musicians and classical dancers, she's had the advantage of getting the right kind of atmosphere since her childhood. However, for art and creativity to bloom, an artist has to possess certain extraordinary inherent qualities rather than just a privileged background to be noticed and celebrated by the world. Arushi's story is an excellent exemplification of this point.

STAR BUD

(Childhood)

An artist is not only born but also raised. Arushi was born into an illustrious family of artists. Her father, Madhup Mudgal and aunt Madhavi Mudgal were already acclaimed artists known for their valuable contributions made in the field of classical music and dance in the country. The Mudgal family's commitment to teaching music and dance started way back in 1939 when Arushi's grandfather Professor Vinaya Chandra Maudgalya, a prominent classical musician from the Gwalior Gharana, opened the Gandharva Mahavidyalaya in Delhi. His aim of starting such a school was to make music and dance accessible to everyone and not just be limited to higher society. Over the years it gained a reputation for being an excellent institution in imparting training in classical dance and music. The baton was later passed to Madhup*ji* by his father. In fact, Arushi's mother, Manisha Mudgal, met her husband when she was learning music at the Mahavidyalaya. The school is now located in Deen Dayal Upadhaya Marg and currently teaches dance and music to around 1200 students.

As a child, Arushi and her sister Sawani (also an accomplished musician) would wake up to the sounds of music and dance. It was natural for both sisters to absorb everything they saw and heard.

A studious child, Arushi excelled in all her subjects and was popular with her teachers. Her artistic traits have been quite apparent since her childhood. She was focused, self-disciplined and a perfectionist, a fact almost everyone—from her sister Sawani to her mother and close friends—has said about her. Even as a child, she liked everything to be just right. She preferred to pack her school bag herself in neat and particular order and usually completed her homework in school itself. Once in class four, she scored 99.5% on her math test, and the young Arushi started crying for losing out on half a per cent, giving us a good idea of her perfectionist character.

A quiet child by nature, Arushi enjoyed burying herself in her novels even when she went to her relatives' homes with her family. Her sister, Sawani, three and a half years older than her, has been a constant friend, with their bond only strengthening over the years. Arushi had a few close friends in school, and she's remained in touch with them even after finishing school. One such friend is Aliya Fatehullah. According to her, it was Arushi's caring nature that helped them become friends. She says:

> "In class seven, I happened to miss the first few weeks of the academic year due to personal reasons. When I joined, only the very front desk was available, so I sat there. A few days later, Arushi returned from a trip and just started casually talking to me. She was the class monitor, and was the one busy talking to me instead of "minding the class". The whole thing was just so remarkable and easy for her, that for someone like me—who was still struggling to find her footing in the new school and being at an insecure stage—having someone just come and speak to you in the most ordinary and casual way was a big deal. Of course, later we realised we are the same kind of 'crazy', and it just grew from there." Aliya further describes Arushi as open, passionate and with a quiet confidence and humility about her artistic capabilities. "It's quite easy to let all the accolades and applause get to you, but she's firmly grounded and always looking for ways to grow", she said. "Her energy is contagious, and she pours herself into whatever she is doing. I don't recall her doing things by half". After school hours, Arushi spent most of her time at the Gandharva Mahavidyalaya, attending classes and practising dance and music with

> other students. "Coming back from school, I would rush to the dance class, and a lot of what I learnt was by observation, watching my aunt practice and create", she disclosed.

Her other friend, Meera, recalled incidents from their childhood, revealing the more mischievous side of her friend. "We used to try not to look at each other during our music classes, because both of us were (and still are) really bad at suppressing our laughter! But invariably something or the other in class would trigger our laughter. And to make the situation worse, I would nudge her, and she would literally cry from laughing too hard! She's intrinsically naughty which is not apparent to most people".

Carving Her Own Path

Arushi was barely five when she started learning dance with her aunt (Madhavi Mudgal). She would crawl into her aunt's practice room and watch her. "I had the inclination for dance always", Arushi said. However, Madhavi*ji* disclosed that she never received any special treatment; she was just like any of her other students. Arushi's love for dance was so great that whenever her aunt would announce a new piece to be taught, or an upcoming show to prepare for, she would jump with excitement and joy.

Her mother, Manisha*ji,* mentioned that Arushi was just as good at music and even composed a *raag* when she was barely five. She said her daughter wrote the notations in detail and named it "*Chandrakala Tara*". In fact, as a child, Arushi was also a member of the children's choir of the Gandharva Mahavidyalaya. It was only when she was in her teens that she shifted her focus entirely to dance, though she continued to sing and participate in the Gandharva choir. Music, for Arushi, has always been the backbone of her dance. Meera Shirodkar, a family friend of Arushi's who learnt music at the Gandharva Mahavidyalaya, mentioned that Arushi was an excellent singer and said, "We attended the music class together. She was very fast at picking up singing". After middle school, Arushi got more involved in dance and started travelling for performances. Her first international performance tour happened in 1999 in Brazil with her aunt as a part of her dance group. That trip gave her a different kind of exposure. She said she absolutely loved the trip. "I was dancing with my Guru and my Guru's Guru, Guru Kelucharan Mohapatra... it was unbelievably exciting for me and overwhelming in a nice way", she said.

Madhavi*ji* beautifully described how Arushi has managed to carve her own dance style. She said, "Learning is by osmosis, and she (Arushi) shows it. The base is mine, but she's bloomed and followed her own style". She went on to praise her for being self-disciplined and independent by nature. "During the Brazil tour, I had other students with me. She wasn't special", she said. "We were staying in an apartment with two different rooms. Arushi was always with her friends—other dancers in the group". However, Madhavi*ji* candidly accepted that she shares a special bond with Arushi. "She feels what I'm saying. I guess that's natural because she's been taught by me from a young age. We do a lot of duets together, and sometimes there are constraints of the stage...she understands immediately".

Blooming with Encouragement and Support

Arushi started performing solo when she was in school. Although she had to miss her classes due to frequent travelling for performances, she still managed to score well in her exams. "There was no pressure from our parents, they always supported us in our decisions", Arushi said, explaining how she managed to do so well academically. She also lovingly acknowledged the encouragement she received from the principal and teachers of Carmel Convent School, where she did her schooling. She recounted:

> When I was in grade eight or nine, I was selected for the Original Mind Award for 'Creativity', which was presented to me by Dr. Murli Manohar Joshi. This happened outside of school, but Sister Nirmalini—my school Headmistress and later Principal—specially came to attend the ceremony. The following day, she announced with pride over the

> intercom informing the entire school about my award. I remember feeling so shy, because everyone in class was looking at me and clapping! But more than that, I remember feeling very emotional at the gesture. I still tear up when I remember such incidents from school. I am deeply attached to my school and all the teachers, and still in touch with most of them.

Harini Kapoor, an ex-student of the Mahavidyalaya and a family friend, also gives us a good impression of Arushi as a child: My earliest memory of Arushi is that of a tiny girl with spectacles and thick hair who would sometimes come down from the fourth floor with her mother, and stand leaning against her at the foot of the stairs on the second floor where we used to have our class in the Gandharva Mahavidyalaya. Eyes wide open, so open that you noticed them through her spectacles, with a quiet sense of wonder on her face, is how I remember her. This must have been around 1990... I had no interaction with her, but I had an impression of this small child as totally unselfconscious, quiet, happy to be with mommy, head tilted, chin cocked up and eyes and ears full of the things she was seeing and hearing. More of an outward-bound child, not absorbed in herself but gathering every stimulus around her.

Arushi had an ideal childhood, loving parents and an enabling environment. While she excelled in her studies, she was inclined towards dance (and music) from a very young age, owing to her nurturing environment. Her love and dedication for her art form have only intensified with time.

Ray Floret

(Youth)

In 2004, fresh out of school, Arushi started teaching dance in Gandharva Mahavidyalaya while continuing to travel and perform with her aunt. This entire experience of teaching and performing at prestigious platforms in India and abroad gave her a sense of achievement. However, she shared that back then, she'd never really thought of it as her profession; she just loved everything about it.

In fact, in school, she'd dabbled with the idea of studying hotel management, becoming an actor, a singer or even a writer. Arushi has enjoyed writing since her school days, and has written articles on several topics related to dance for various magazines. A few years ago, she also co-authored a book titled *The Bud and the Blossom,* on the aesthetics of *Odissi*, along with the senior aesthetician, Prof. S.K. Saxena. Apart from this, she has even conceptualized and written a short script on honour killing for a Netflix anthology. Things just fell into place for her, and she kept following (and greatly enjoying) the path that beckoned her.

Juggling Two Lives

After completing her senior secondary schooling successfully, Arushi joined Lady Shri Ram College for B.A. (Hons.) in Sociology, a subject she enjoyed. The faculty at LSR was amazing, she said. However, during her first-year college exams, she had to tour France with her aunt and only managed to appear for one of the papers. She was promoted to second year on the condition that she would take both years' papers together at the end of the year. However, she had to travel to Europe again in April and May that year and missed her exams yet again. Also, by then, she had invested too much into dance and had started performing solos. She said she was always in a rush and had no time for anything except dance and her studies. At one point, things became so hectic that Arushi finally had to drop out of college to focus entirely on dance. After this, she ended up completing her graduation through correspondence. When Arushi was not on tour, she was busy practising and perfecting her dance form and had little time for anything else. Consequently, she wasn't very social in this phase of her life. She says:

> Once, while still in college, I went out with my college friends to a café and kept looking at my watch, because, I didn't want to miss my dance class. I was so occupied with dance that I didn't get time to hang out with friends or do the regular things that people my age did. But I was

> very happy doing what I did, and have no regrets. In fact, the amount of hours that I put into my practice at that time was crucial, and laid the foundation on which my dance stands today.

She also added, “Besides, my friendships happen on tours. I like organic connections. It takes an effort for me to go out of the way to socialize, unlike my sister who is the exact opposite of me in this regard”. The two sisters are “extremely protective” of each other, said their mother. Despite her hectic schedule and being away from home for months, Arushi was still a normal girl eager to experience life. Devika, another childhood friend of hers, said that she relates to Arushi a lot. They’re both their true selves with each other and enjoy doing simple and even silly things together. “Before I moved to Israel, I used to live in Bombay, in Juhu. Arushi came to visit me in 2012 or 2013. It was a general chill trip. We stayed at home, made mango shakes and went for walks. She became friends with the neighbours in the building. On one of the evenings, we went to see the play “Piya Behrupia” at Prithvi theatre, and it had Namit Das, the “Wake-up Sid” actor...we silently crushed on him and exchanged giggles like teenagers. After the play, we devised a plan to approach and impress him but chickened out when it came to executing it.”

Family Support

Arushi’s sister Sawani, who sometimes travels together with Arushi and their aunt’s group for tours, said that they have a lot of fun on trips, visiting places, shopping, and trying out the local cuisine. “We really enjoy each other’s company. Arushi hates shopping, but on tours, I forcefully drag her along”, Sawani said, laughing.

Arushi’s family has been her pillar of support. She says that all four of them (she, her sister and her parents) are extremely close to each other. She has nothing but praise for them, and says:

“My parents are simple and pure souls. As transparent as one can be. My mom has this aura of warmth, and my dad is simple and honest. They’ve taught me to be honest and simple and give my hundred per cent to work. My sister and I crack jokes with our parents as we would with our friends. I have this huge advantage because of being born into such an illustrious family, and initially, perhaps opportunities came my way, but they were only maintained because I worked hard. I have never taken things for granted. Choosing the family that we are born into is not in our hands, but what we do after being born into it is. I am someone who believes in action. So instead of either becoming complacent due to my lineage, or being pressurized by the weight of it, I choose to work consistently and revel in the bliss of my art and creativity. I feel satisfied and proud of the achievements that came my way because I put in those extra hours into my work. There may be people around you, but as an artist, you alone have to pave your path; it's a solitary journey." There is a quiet confidence about her, which seems to stem from her honesty towards her art.

FULL BLOOM

(Present)

WORLDWIDE FAME AND RECOGNITION

Life has never moved as planned for this amazing young artist. It was a gradual journey fueled by her love for the traditional dance form and an enabling environment. "Before I knew it, I was doing it", she said. While still in school, Arushi was already being recognised for her talent. She had been awarded the Bal Shri award by the Govt. of India, given by the former Indian President, Shri Abdul Kalam. In 2008, Arushi was invited by the famous dancer-choreographer Pina Bausch of Wuppertal Tanz Theater to perform at the Internationals Tanz Festival in Dusseldorf, Germany. She also performed at Theatre de la Ville, Paris and various other cities in France, Belgium and Austria as part of a recital named 'Famille Mudgal', and the Fall for Dance Festival in New York and Los Angeles, USA as well. She was awarded the first Touring Fellowship by Milapfest, UK, for 2010-11. She toured different cities of the UK in May 2011, giving highly appreciated performances and conducting workshops. By her mid-twenties, her fame had already spread far and wide nationally and internationally. However, despite her spectacular achievements and popularity, Arushi has remained grounded. "I take the fame in my stride...Humility is a value I've learnt from my family, and I would like to hold on to it. When I see my parents beaming, I feel proud", she said. "Thanks to art, it holds you and keeps you going".

THE CHALLENGES OF BEING AN ARTIST

When asked about the challenges that one faces in the field of classical Indian dance, Arushi believes that like every other profession, this too has its own battles. "Art is not an easy field. You must take it up only if you are truly passionate about it and happy to dance despite the challenges. There is no guarantee of any returns whatsoever. It is not like a regular job where you earn a certain fixed income every month. For upcoming artists who do not come from supportive families, it can become a real challenge. Besides, a lot of people, even today, do not realise that dance can be someone's main profession in life. And while the mindset has evolved, there is still a long way to go. There is also the problem of unprofessionalism, whether it is on the artist's part or the organizer's."

She added, "When people understand but simply don't care enough, it frustrates me. There are infrastructural issues at times, like a problem with the stage or lights. I am sure other dancers will relate to this. I have stepped on a nail while dancing on stage, and have had to rush for a tetanus shot post-performance. And it has happened more than once". Yet she smiled and continued:

"But the intangible return that the arts bless us with makes it all worth it. It is a sense of freedom from the world that dance provides; a flight I find in the comforts of its wings and there alone. It has healing and nurturing powers, and all problems pale in front of the joy that one experiences while dancing. Thus, you keep reminding yourself to let go, to not be troubled by things that are not in your control. It's a process." Arushi also spoke about the role of Vidushi Leela Samson in her life, who is a world-renowned Bharatanatyam dancer, and a dear friend of the Mudgal family. "I look up to her. In execution, things can go wrong. Stage lights can go off at a crucial moment, for example. But letting go in art is an art itself. Leela akka has this quality of letting go of all the external factors and channeling her focus on her art, on or off stage. I try to learn and pick up these things from her". About maintaining her relationships, Arushi said, "Art becomes a medium of connecting with people. Paths cross, we learn from every experience and move on. Meeting and interacting with different people, sharing their joys and sorrows; this makes my experience of life fuller and richer, and further enhances my relationship with dance. Therefore, I value all my connections". Speaking about the struggles in life, she said: "I believe in counting my blessings, and there are many! Nevertheless, one is bound to experience all sorts of emotions in life, and it cannot be happy all the time. There are moments of pain, anger, disillusionment, and frustration in every individual's life. But it's what we take away from these moments that defines us. I find that the moments of resistance in my life have helped me grow not only as a human, but also as an artist. It has made my understanding of characters and their layered emotions nuanced, thereby making my expression more honest. Thus, I am grateful for every moment of my life, because, it has shaped me and my artistic sensibilities. I try to bring the essence (of all my experiences) into my art." Devika also spoke about this sensitive side of her friend. She said Arushi reminds her of soft clay: gentle, soft and mouldable. "When she experiences life, she waits, she feels, and emulates. When I saw her performing solo for the first time, I realised that she, may be knowingly, uses all of these sensitivities to express her dance form. It was heartwarming and it made me smile for how her personality is tailor-made for the craft she's a part of". Arushi reflects:

Life has its own ways of nourishing you. If it puts you in a spot, it also takes you out from it. With time, you realise that it is all part of a larger scheme of things, where everything has a role to play, and yet nothing really matters. It's all maya. So, I am slowly learning to pause and appreciate the simple joys of life—a beautiful conversation, watching the sunset, exchanging smiles with strangers, enjoying my sister's recipes—these things enthuse me with positivity.

POST-PANDEMIC LIFE

The Covid lockdown put a stop to her tours, but her daily home routine remained the same. Her mother, Manisha*ji,* disclosed that during the lockdown, Arushi took it upon herself to keep an account of everything, including the Vidyalaya work. She credited her daughter for managing things extremely well. Arushi also came up with different creative ideas and started working on them during the lockdown. "There is an urge within me to create. To see the journey of an intangible idea take shape gradually, layer by layer and eventually become a work of art…it is *the* most fulfilling experience for me. It is hard to put it in words, the satisfaction is inexplicable," she said. Arushi is currently performing, writing about dance, teaching online classes and workshops, and creating choreographies based on different texts and ideas. Choreography is not new to her. Her first choreography was in 2005 in the UK. She said that she learnt the tools of choreography by observing her aunt Madhavi*ji*, who is a "brilliant choreographer". Studying dance is something she's deeply inclined towards. Her enthusiasm was apparent when she said, "I want to create more work. I'm back in the zone, driven and ready to dive in!".

Arushi's inborn talent, along with her passion, dedication and continuous exposure has ensured that even at a young age she's mastered her art form. And yet she remains untouched by it all. As her friend Meera puts it succinctly, "it is a rare quality not to get comfortable with herself. As she grows, her art has also grown".

2

Choiti Ghosh

Object Theatre Artist & Puppeteer

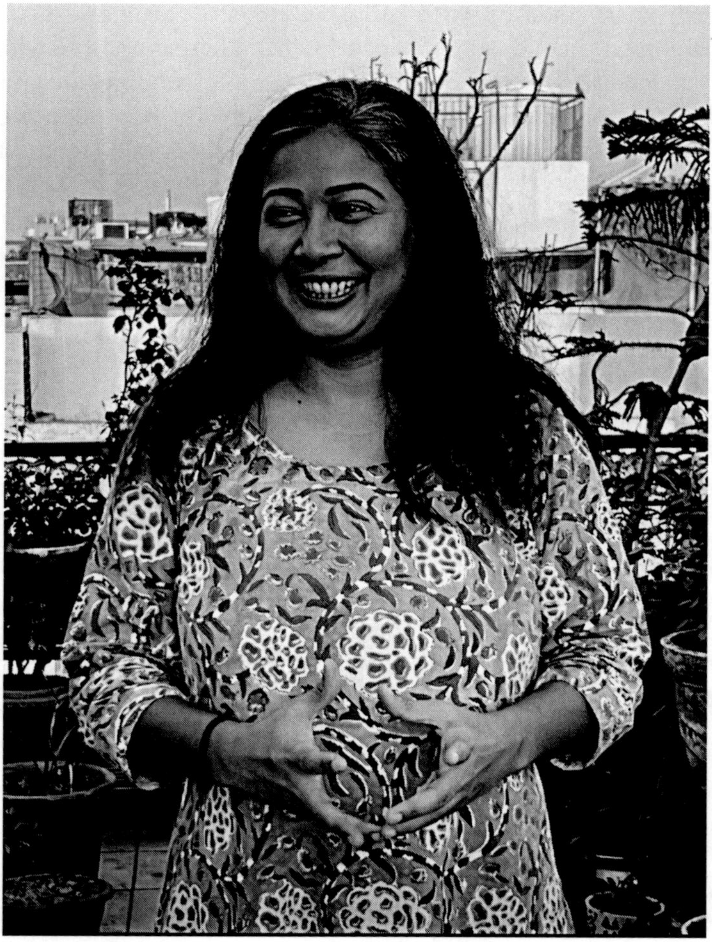

Figure 2

"It's the kind of theatre that de-centers human beings from the center of the universe."

—Choiti Ghosh

Choiti Ghosh (b. 1980) is India's first and possibly only Object Theatre artist. She's also an acclaimed puppeteer, actor, singer, writer, and artistic director of the Mumbai and Delhi-based Object Theatre company called Tram Arts Trust.

Choiti is admired and respected for her unique area of work and has won multiple national awards, including the prestigious Sahitya Rangabhoomi Vinod Doshi Fellowship for Outstanding Young Artists in 2011 and the Ustad Bismillah Khan Yuva Puraskar given by Sangeet Natak Akademi in 2016. Her plays have been performed at major festivals, venues, educational institutions and alternative spaces all over India, as well as at festivals in Germany, the US, Sri Lanka, and Japan. As a director, she has been invited to France (Theatre Gerard Phillippe, Paris), Germany (ASSITEJ Germany Directors Gathering, Berlin) and the UK (British Council India Showcase delegate) to share her artistic practices.

What's interesting about her artistic journey is that she's had an unusual childhood filled with plenty of travel and creative experiments. She was introduced to Jatra plays by her grandfather, who had founded a Jatra company in Delhi in 1980-81. Choiti performed for the first time in 1983, when she was barely three. Soon after, she started appearing in her family's Jatra plays as a child artist. Over the years, she has worked as a performer and singer with some of India's leading directors and theatre companies like Naya Theatre (Bhopal) under Dr. Habib Tanvir, Jana Natya Manch (Delhi), ANANT (Delhi) under her father, Dr. Ashish Ghosh, Katkatha Puppet Arts Trust (Delhi) under the direction of Anurupa Roy, Arpana Theatre (Mumbai) under the direction of Sunil Shanbag and Q Theatre Productions (Mumbai), among many others.

Choiti found her actual calling very late in her life. She was already in her thirties when she finally realised what she wanted to do, and since then, she has dedicated all her time to the practice, research and dissemination of Object Theatre in India. Her incredible story will give readers a glimpse of the person Choiti was before she became an established artist in a field still in its nascent stage in the country (and even around the world). Readers will also get an insight into her creative mind and gain an understanding of how she uses it to communicate innovative ideas and give meaning to ordinary objects.

STAR BUD

(Childhood)

The traits of a creative person are visible from a young age if one knows what to look for. However, Choiti displayed tendencies opposite to what one would expect from creative people. On one hand, she was a shy recluse, and on the other, a rebel. At home, she was boisterous, always experimenting, learning new things, and engaging with her environment, often getting into mischief with her close friends.

Until age six, Choiti led a semi-nomadic life, travelling with her parents and performing in her family's *Jatra* plays. While her parents, Ashish and Ruma Ghosh, had different day jobs, they were both still passionate artists at heart. It was inevitable that their only child took to the theatre like a fish takes to water. In fact, her father started a children's theatre group called ANANT, and from the very beginning, Choiti was involved and played different roles in their productions.

LEADING A DOUBLE-LIFE

When Choiti turned six, she was admitted to a mission school in Delhi. As a carefree child whose home environment allowed her to do things her way, Choiti found it difficult to grow accustomed to the instructive and structured school environment. She was an above-average student and, apart from Mathematics, did extremely well in her studies, with English and Social Science being her favourite subjects. Yet, she says that her school life was a "period of anxiety" for her, and she saw herself as a "misfit".

In school, she found a natural ally in her English teacher, Deepti Gulati, who saw the spark in her and encouraged her to realise her potential. Her favourite teacher's loving presence was comforting for Choiti. She was also a great singer from a young age. In class ten, she proposed to do a group song for the school's Teacher's Day function, and her teacher supported her. Otherwise reserved in school, Choiti said she wasn't sure what prompted her to take the initiative, but once she'd made up her mind, she went ahead and gave it her best. It was a popular but bold song, "Man Smart, Woman Smarter", showing Choiti's feminist (and rebellious) streak. After that event, her popularity in school grew, and she started to make friends. However, despite these small achievements that helped her discover other sides of her personality, she continued to be a recluse in school.

At home, the scenario was completely opposite. Choiti had a bunch of friends, with many of them performing in her father's *Jatra* plays like her. Joyoti Roy was one such friend, and the two were always involved in mischief. Once, they created a toilet paper film, drawing figures and images on toilet rolls and cajoling their mothers, relatives and friends to watch it. The story was rolled down from the top of a bed, requiring one of them to sit and hold it while the other had to gently unfold it while sitting under the bed. They charged the viewers a rupee per show, and they continued this for a few days until they found another equally engaging game. Another funny childhood memory Choiti recalled was how, together with her group of friends, she would constantly look for abandoned houses in their locality to convert them into a club for their different activities. For months, they kept searching for such houses and even identified a few dilapidated buildings, but they were either chased away by guards or thought they were haunted and dropped the idea altogether.

Shweta Majumdar, another good friend of Choiti's, spoke about a side of her friend that she said was apparent to her even as a child. She said that Choiti was intuitive as a child and always in touch with her feelings. "One day we were sitting together on Choiti's terrace, and she was talking about something when I became keenly aware of her ability to put her exact feelings into words".

Joyoti, Shweta and Choiti mostly spent time together after school and remained busy with fun and offbeat activities like running a mobile library or forming a dog rescue team to rescue stray dogs, and even indulged in midnight feasting from time to time. "There was a permissiveness around our friendship, because, we were neighbours and our parents knew each other well", Shweta said. Thus, while Choiti lacked friends in school and was seen as an introverted child, she was the exact opposite in her home environment.

Choiti was also an athlete, and at the age of thirteen, during a regular medical checkup, she was mistreated and abused by an external doctor. While some action was taken against the person, the issue wasn't satisfactorily resolved. She disclosed that, in hindsight, the negative impact of this event could have been another reason for her reclusive and inhibited demeanour in school. Choiti's mother, Ruma Ghosh—an acclaimed theatre artist herself—said that she became aware that her daughter was facing "some issues" at her new school but thought of them as teething problems that Choiti would be able to "negotiate" with time.

Ruma*ji* also shared that Choiti's pre-schooling started at her father's school, which he'd started in their neighbourhood, intending to promote vernacular language as the medium of education. After that, she was transferred to Sarada Mission in class one and completed her primary education there. Her daughter's creative streak had become apparent to her from a very young age, as apart from acting in her family's folk theatre plays, she also used to paint, write, and sing. When she changed schools, Choiti lost touch with painting but continued writing and singing.

BEING MISUNDERSTOOD

Choiti was transferred to a new school when she was around ten. It was in this school that she started facing problems and became "reticent". However, Ruma*ji* also disclosed that as a mother, she knew that Choiti had much more to her personality than was apparent to her teachers and others. Unfortunately, very few could recognize this side of her personality in this school. A lot depends on teachers and peers to bring out the hidden talent of a child. In that respect, Mrs. Deepti Gulati and a couple of other teachers played a major role in influencing and motivating her to open up and explore different interests while at school. While reminiscing, Mrs. Gulati said that Choiti was one of her "best and most lovable students; she always had something different to say in my class". Another teacher, Mrs. Kamala Menon, seemed equally proud of her ex-student:

> In a class of 35 children, to remember one who loved to draw and fill out maps and made an effort to write beautifully is not at all hard. Choiti was a little girl with an even temper and usually stayed quiet in class, but excelled in the work she submitted. Choiti took a lot of interest in looking at the maps and copying them neatly, and could actually locate places just after going through the lesson once. This graphic ability of hers was a very happy experience for me, especially when most students in her class marked the river Ganga somewhere in Tamil Nadu.

However, Choiti's Political Science teacher from class twelve, Mrs. Madhu Juneja, said that she was aware of Choiti's discomfort in the school environment. "There was something out-of-the-box about her thinking and she had an independent viewpoint and very convincing arguments. She also had a soft and sensitive demeanour, probably related to her creative side", she said.

Thus, it was Choiti's parents, together with her close set of friends, and a few of her teachers, that discovered the different shades of her personality and her artistic bent of mind, and made it somewhat easy for her to endure school life.

The direction she eventually chose as an artist was completely a different one, requiring a growth mindset. Her mistakes, failures and challenges helped her uncover her vast potential and eventually led her to find her unique personal language as an artist.

RAY FLORET
(Youth)

Choiti's college life was in total contrast to what she'd experienced as a school student. After finishing school, Choiti joined the prestigious St. Stephens College, where she completed her B.A. (Hons) in English, a subject she greatly enjoyed throughout her school years. In fact, some of her favourite stories from that time inspired her to craft unique Object Theatre plays later in life.

In college, more than fifty per cent of her classmates were artists, and she knew many of her college seniors from school. This worked to her advantage; she had already acted in some school plays with them, and they were aware of her talent. Moreover, there was an active theatre society in college, and she soon became a member. All these little positive developments made her feel she'd finally "found freedom".

Together with her college friends, Jennifer, John, Shayoni and a few others, Choiti performed in many college plays. In fact, Jennifer described her as someone with a "creative force". "We studied English Literature together at St. Stephen's College from 1998-2001. In the three years that we were there, Choiti was involved in a spate of plays, taking part in the annual and mid-term productions, and she was a part of the College's Shakespeare Society. I remember sitting on the terrace at her house on balmy Delhi nights watching rehearsals, or discussing scenes and reading plays with endless cups of liquor chai", Jennifer said.

Finding her Purpose

Choiti also continued to be involved with ANANT as a performer and singer during this period. Apart from her performances in college, she also produced and performed several plays with her father's theatre company. It was only in college that it became clear to Choiti that doing theatre was more than just a fun activity for her, and that she would like to pursue it professionally too. Of course, like anyone else, Choiti had also toyed with the idea of becoming a writer, an academic, a journalist, a filmmaker, a film actress and even a *Baul* singer at different points in her life. However, as she became more involved with theatre, it became apparent to her where she was headed. And yet, she wasn't fully satisfied with the path she had been following so far as a performing artist. She continued to experiment and look for new ways to express herself. After completing college, Choiti even applied to NSD. However, she soon realised that she wasn't cut out for it and left it during the selection process, before submitting her final project. She said:

> There were more suitable candidates who wanted and deserved to be there much more than me, and tried much harder than me, I guess. I still didn't know what kind of theatre I wanted to do, but I knew I would have to keep looking for it elsewhere. Funnily enough, I now teach Object Theatre at NSD sometimes, as a visiting faculty. It was a blessing in disguise.

It was in the 2000s that a young and freshly graduated Choiti started experimenting with different forms of theatre. Apart from performing and managing her father's theatre, she also started performing with other prestigious theatre groups like Naya Theatre, Katkatha Puppet Arts Trust and Sunil Shanbag (on *Mastana Rampuri*).

Life-Changing Moments

Two significant events happened in her life during this period, which helped her grow as a person and as an artist. Firstly, she met her future husband, Abhisar Bose, a documentary film-maker, while working for Naya Theatre. Abhisar was handling theatre production for the Bhopal-based theatre company at that point in time. They first met as colleagues, lost touch for years before reconnecting in Mumbai, and finally married in 2014. Choiti calls Abhisar her "rock" and credits him for bringing in a semblance of order in her life. Also, because of his experience and technical expertise, all her theatre production work is handled by him. She also accepted that while he adds great value to her work, she's unable to reciprocate the same. "To help him with his kind of work, one needs to have technical knowledge and experience", she elaborated. Abhisar, on his part, too, was full of praise for his wife. "Choiti is a fun-loving, strong-headed, focused and independent person.

She is very passionate about her work, and I must say her communication skills are very strong". About his role in his wife's theatre company, he said:

> I have learnt a lot from her. As the production-in-charge in Tram Arts, I help with photography, videography, creating posters for the plays, video editing and even backstage production. It's fun to work with her. We did so many projects and tours together, from developing the plays to performing for the audience. Our entire team is fun to work with. In fact, for her recent project on Dolls of West Bengal, we toured many interior villages of Sunderbans, travelling throughout and staying on a boat on the huge rivers of the Sundarban delta. It was a new and thrilling experience.

Another pivotal point in her creative journey came when Choiti met Anurupa Roy, the dynamic founder of Katkatha Puppet Arts Trust, Delhi, in 2004. Anurupa approached her for a play and ended up training her in puppetry. Choiti is immensely thankful to Anurupa for introducing her to this art form, allowing her to add a new dimension to her work. Puppetry is not the same as Object Theatre, yet it helped her realise that out of all the work she had done so far, she enjoyed puppet theatre the most. More importantly, she only discovered Object Theatre because she was practising puppet theatre. Choiti continues to collaborate with Katkatha every once in a while.

Anurupa said she connects deeply with Choiti as they started off only a few years apart, and their creative journeys and struggles have been similar. As an artist, she appreciates certain qualities in Choiti. "Choiti is tenacious, has patience and has a sense of community. She understands that an obscure art form such as Object Theatre or puppetry needs the involvement of the larger community. You can't do it alone". Anurupa also revealed that while Choiti is a perfectionist and extremely good with production set-up, she also has a fun side to her and is the most fun person to have during a tour. "She makes you see the lighter side of life".

Her college friend Jennifer highlighted the importance of Choiti's work with Anurupa's company, and how it helped her slowly transition from being a stage actor to an Object Theatre artist. "Choiti's work at Katkatha Puppet Theatre Group after college was perhaps her first time performing on stage but not as an actor. The new perspective this gave her has surely impacted her later work as an Object Theatre artist".

By her late twenties, Choiti had not only grown artistically, but there were changes seen in her personality too. From a reserved child, she'd grown into an assertive and tenacious person who was also a team player and fun to be around.

Full Bloom

(Present)

By the time Choiti hit her thirties, she was already a well-known name as an actor, singer and puppeteer. However, she remained restless and found Actors' Theatre less exciting. It was around this time that she first heard about Object Theatre—a unique performing arts form with its roots in Europe. Object Theatre uses everyday objects as symbols to convey ideas and stories. Choiti became curious about the art form and started reading up on it, unaware that she'd already embarked on a creative journey that she would follow for "the rest of her life".

In 2010, she applied for a month-long workshop at Institut International de la Marionnette in France, and was chosen as one of the fifteen international artists for the workshop (and the only one from India). It was an intensive training course taught by Agnes Limbos, one of Belgium's foremost artists and one of the global stalwarts of Object Theatre. Choiti said she had a really tough time at the workshop, and her mentor was not too impressed by her initially.

Agnes shared that there were sixty artists who had applied for her three-week workshop, but she chose only fifteen out of those. She disclosed that Choiti, along with another girl from Iran, were chosen because of their backgrounds in traditional puppetry. "It was not easy for her. Choiti is a thinking person and is constantly questioning herself", Agnes said. "It took her a week to even understand the vocabulary I was using in the workshop…but slowly she changed and connected to the object. By watching other students, she learnt a lot".

However, the feedback she got from Agnes for her first few assignments was below average. Choiti had to go through an unlearning process before accepting and becoming comfortable with her new learning environment. In fact, Choiti disclosed that she was not fully satisfied with herself, but completed her training under the able guidance of her mentor and learnt by working with the other artists in the group.

However, her real learning started only after she returned to India and started applying what she had been taught into practice. She also took pains to familiarise herself with the French language. "I had to sit with a dictionary and translator to be able to read books on Object Theatre which were mostly in French", she said.

"After returning from the training, I vividly remember Choiti telling me that she felt she had finally found her calling. I think that for her to decide on a niche under the range of theatre that she has been exposed to, especially at a time when Object Theatre was not really being practised in India, must require conviction and also a whole lot of courage", Jennifer said.

Initial Struggles

As the first Object Theatre artist in the country, there were different kinds of challenges she had to face during her initial years. "I was the only practitioner in the country and had to build everything from scratch". She started crafting stories for children and young people using everyday household objects. "My focus and effort went into creating Object Theatre. Fifty per cent of our work is for children and the rest is for adults. Theatre, for very early young children is a recent phenomenon, and we have so far created only one production for them", she said. "Also, I have been battling the misconception that Object Theatre is only for children right from the beginning". During this time, Choiti also took up odd jobs to keep herself financially stable. Most of her earnings came from teaching theatre students and doing workshops with educational institutions rather than from performances. She continued to perform in her old plays but started refusing fresh work as she knew she'd finally found the specific form she wanted to express herself in as an artist.

Agnes shared that many years later, she went to watch one of Choiti's shows in Europe and immensely enjoyed the play. However, later she explained to Choiti that "Object Theatre is not only for children, but also for responsible adults. That playfulness with objects can also be applied to serious subjects".

Finding Firm Ground

In 2011, Choiti set up her theatre company, Tram Arts Trust, along with some of her close friends. It was under Tram that she put up her first Object Theatre performance, *Nostos*. Based on Homer's *Odyssey*, her performance was staged as part of the Prithvi Theatre Carnival, and it received a great response. She said it was her second Object Theatre production in 2011, *Bird's Eye View,* not only did well but also firmly established her as an Object Theatre artist. The plays they've done are largely nonverbal, using objects found in daily life, with the storytelling aimed at stimulating the senses. "You're not only teaching yourself but also creating an ecosystem", Choiti explained. Over the years, Choiti has produced several successful (and unsuccessful) plays for people of all ages and continues to work with new ideas around Object Theatre. She accepts that she's met some failures, but they did not deter her. "Object Theatre changes people's point of view. It decentralizes the human body". One of Choiti's aims with Object Theatre has been to challenge the belief that human beings are the most important entity in this universe. "You're one of many. It's not an easy change of perception", she said. However, her tenacity and passion for her work help her to keep moving in her self-chosen direction.

Choiti's latest project, which in her own as well as her mother's words is a "humongous project that will take a lifetime", is about traditional objects. Earlier, her plays were around everyday objects and had a somewhat Western influence. Over the years, there has been a natural and gradual movement towards researching theatre with objects in the Indian context, and this has been more prominent in the last few productions. The current Dolls project consciously engages only with traditional objects. "Objects speak a lot about us as a society and culture. They're a window through which you look at the world. And so, the recent project is an exploration of our culture and contexts", she specified. She has managed to procure some funds for the performance. However, a large part of the project involves extensive research and travel, which is so far self-funded.

Talking about her struggles as the founder of Tram Arts Trust, Choiti said that theatre artists in India are the "most enterprising people". They start with nothing and have no expectations or surety of how things will shape up in the future, and yet they dedicate their life to perfecting their art and manage to make "money stretch". In that sense, she said that she's no different from other artists as she has learnt to "rise up to the challenges".

Choiti's artistic journey not only involved many creative experiments but also required her to have the courage, conviction, and perseverance to keep going on her chosen path till she finally found her specific form of expression as an artist.

Karan Talwar, one of the board members of Tram Arts Trust and a close friend of Choiti's who knows her work intimately, said:

Choiti and her chosen form of Object Theatre were either not understood, or just ignored by large swathes of people in the theatre. This is understandable in a country obsessed with commercial fanfare. I recall Choiti going through waves of existentialism as an artist, questioning her choices...but in the end, sticking with her gut feeling. She persevered and simply kept doing what she felt was right for her as an artist. There were many instances of rejection she had to face in this time, and no judgement here on people who were inadvertently making her feel like this. Everyone is trying to simply survive and be sustainable, and often, experimental fringe forms don't find space or economics. Choiti was well-established in Indian and International theatre circles and could have easily gone back to a kind of theatre which already has an ecosystem, but she didn't. Now, ten years down, she has ended up creating almost a 'first generation' of Object Theatre. The form has crawled its way into popular productions. So many practitioners have attended her workshops and her shows. Her children's workshops have enabled new ways of viewing theatre. It sounds like a fairytale story about a light at the end, but in reality, the struggle still persists. But she stays true to her chosen form, and that is just so inspiring and something I really look up to her for.

Choiti's journey as an Object Theatre artist might be still young, but she's successfully navigated through various challenges and covered miles. She continues to add value to society through her unique work as she goes about setting up and popularizing the "Indian Object Theatre."

3

Hina Siddiqui

Queer, Neurodivergent Transmedia Storyteller & Theatre Maker

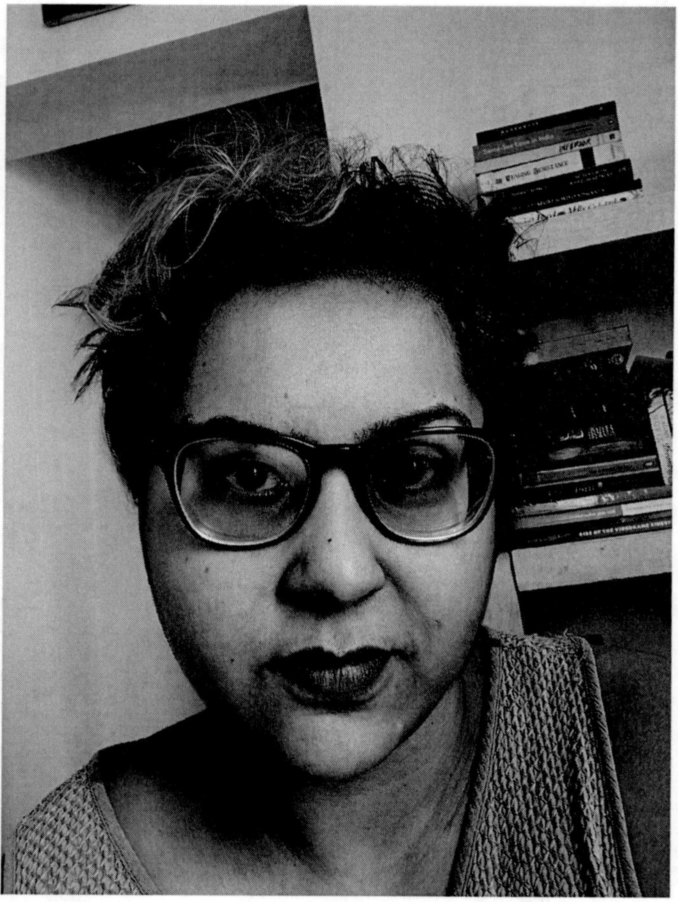

Figure 3

"Theatre was my catharsis. I had to process my emotions in a theatrical space because I didn't know where else to do it."

—Hina Siddiqui

HINA SIDDIQUI (b. 1986) is a Queer, Neurodivergent Transmedia Storyteller. Currently, she makes games, writes comics, runs a newsletter and podcast, and conducts sex-ed programmes for young people. She firmly believes in queering storytelling for the future, and has written numerous plays, fiction pieces, vignettes, story documentations, essays, and articles from that viewpoint. Hina also has extensive experience in making theatre with communities, where her focus is on creating spaces where fantasies and lived realities can be shared and witnessed. In fact, she started her creative journey as the Artist Leader—writing, performing, and directing plays at Orchestrated Q'Works—a Pune-based theatre collective she founded. It was the first performance-making collective to include transwomen and anyone who identified as a woman.

Hina holds a Professional Certificate in Performance & Training from the London Academy of Music and Dramatic Art. She was an ARThink South Asia (ATSA) Fellow 2016–17, where she completed a secondment at the Spill International Festival, UK. She was also awarded a Seed Grant by the Association for Women's Rights in Development (AWID)—a global, feminist, movement-support organisation—in 2017 to develop a programme for mental health and the arts in collaboration with the Red Dot Foundation. She has also represented India at the Women Playwrights International Conference and the Contact International Forum in Manchester, and was featured in Key City Theatre's International Playwrights line-up in Washington.

In 2019, she joined Gyan Adab, one of the most established arts and contemporary cultural spaces in Pune. At Gyaan Adab, Hina spearheaded arts and learning programmes for the community through the support of local artists and even started an arts festival called 'The Heroine's Journey'. Her ultimate goal is to develop a community-driven transmedia studio that tells the stories of people in different ways through multiple media and platforms.

STAR BUD

(Childhood)

Hina was born in a lower-middle-class family in Pune, Maharashtra. Her father, Fahim Siddiqui, worked in goods transportation for a while. He also worked for bookies at the RWITC Pune racecourse.

Her mother, Poornima, was mainly a French teacher and still continues to teach. Hina has a sister, Subuhi, who is seven years older than her. Her parents' story is like a slice-of-life Bollywood film. She revealed that while her father is a Muslim, her mother is a Hindu from Mauritius who came to Pune to study. Poornima*ji* met her now-husband at a Christmas party. "My mom's roommate and Dad's best friend were dating. They needed a double for a Christmas party entry, and each of them dragged their respective friends along", said Hina. "The two went out again for the New Year's party that year and a few months later ended up marrying each other".

While their story is certainly romantic, their marriage also caused a furore on both sides of the family. In fact, Poornima*ji*'s father greatly disapproved of her marriage, and there was a big showdown where he asked his daughter to choose between her family and her new husband. Poornima*ji* chose the latter, and as a consequence, her father severed all ties with her, not contacting her even once for the next two decades. It was during the marriage of Poornima*ji*'s youngest brother that the whole family—including her two younger brothers and a younger sister—reunited, and Hina met her maternal grandfather for the first time. Hina's paternal grandfather was a scriptwriter in the Hindi film industry. "There are stories of all kinds of famous people eating at the house I grew up in", she said. However, he passed away when her dad was in class five, and her grandmother raised her three boys singlehandedly (her eldest son passed away at a young age). "She was quite unconventional and strong for her time". Hina spent her childhood in a single-room 'chawl-like' house—a pre-independence house located in the camp area of Pune—with her family comprising her parents, sister, and paternal grandmother. Their living condition was in complete contrast to the lifestyle of her mother's family. "I've seen the house my mother was born in. She grew up in a bungalow with gardens and fields. I remember when people from Mauritius or distant relatives came visiting, it was a matter of embarrassment that we lived in a tiny house in a not-so-prosperous neighbourhood".

Hina was an amicable child. Her mother described her as being 'non-fussy' about everything, and always ready to help her with household chores. "I still remember the day I was leaving the nursing home after her birth. There was a slight drizzle outside. I took it as The Almighty showering his blessings upon my little bundle of joy", said Poornima*ji*. "Till today, I believe that Hina is a 'Gift' from the Almighty. Her intellect and creative accomplishments are not inherited, but a gift she was born with". Hina's parents and others around her saw her as an easy-going, happy child, but Hina was living in a world of her own. "A large part of my childhood is a blank because I was living in my head", she said. "I was always in this universe where I was able to control the narrative as opposed to this world. I was living in a dissociative state. The official psychological diagnosis for my dissociation is maladaptive daydreaming—something I only got to know in recent years".

Emotional Struggles

Hina started Nursery in a convent school. Her sister Subuhi was also studying in the same school. On her first day, Hina was dropped off at school by her dad, but half an hour later, little Hina was back home all by herself as she was overwhelmed by the school environment and missing home. Her school was at least a 10-minute walk. Hina's father was at home at that time and was alarmed to see his daughter back home unaccompanied. He took her back to school and fired the teachers for their negligence. Hina said this wasn't the first time she'd done something like that. She'd run away from home on multiple occasions. She was barely three when she ran away from her house the first time. She recounted:

> My mom had had a difficult delivery, and the baby did not survive. She was quite unwell. The adults in the house were busy, and there was no one supervising me. I escaped my home and walked down to this Udupi restaurant about five hundred meters away from the house where my parents used to take me sometimes. I ordered something to eat, broke a glass and ran out, scared that I would be reprimanded. That is when my people found me. This is an attribute of autistic children. They do not know how to express discomfort or disengagement; they just leave the place. I continue to physically exit overwhelming or overstimulating situations even now. I think it has served me well in avoiding a lot of potential abuse, but at the same time has thrown me into some odd realities as well. This habit of disengagement is not a conscious decision. It's like how people instinctively pull their hands away from a flame. My body takes me away from situations where my mind senses like it's under attack.

However, throughout her childhood and a big part of her adult life, Hina was unable to process her emotions or the disengagement she felt at times with people around her. It was only in 2021, after a mental breakdown, that Hina found out about her neurodivergency through online testing and understood the reasons behind her past behaviour. She also informed her parents of the same. "When things get too loud, I get disturbed. I also experience shutdown, which is another mental state associated with autism and ADHD. I didn't know that in my childhood. I thought I had to bear it", she said.

Hina was an average student. Studies were inconsequential to her. She also didn't have too many friends. "'Friend' is a hard word for me to figure out. I had difficult connections with human beings. You're always consciously performing what is expected of you. I met some great people in school...but I was always masking and never connected to them", she said. The narrative Hina projected in school was that she lived in a massive bungalow. She'd based her story on a house owned by close friends of her parents that her family regularly visited. "It was an opulent space with chandeliers and fireplaces and gardens and big doors", she said. While her sister, Subuhi, was comfortable and "knew the manners", Hina felt disconnected and like a misfit in that space. "I was this wild little thing who was perpetually saying things that didn't make sense. I sounded like I was misbehaving and throwing tantrums. I have very vivid memories of that place but not fond memories". Hina used her memories of the bungalow to create the house she lived in and described it to her classmates, giving them the impression that she came from a wealthy family. She would wait for the school to be empty before walking back to her own house. Friends were never invited home, and on the few occasions that some friends saw her in her house or visited her, she would lie to them, telling them that the house belonged to her paternal grandmother, who refused to live with them (in their bungalow) because of her emotional attachment to the old house. Hina was fair, tall and an eloquent communicator, so no one saw through her mental challenges. "If you sound smart and capable, no one tries to look deeper…that's where the understanding of the world ends. People don't think you have a problem", said Hina.

Despite her difficulty connecting with others, Hina did make a few good friends in school with whom she used to hang out. "I would go to their houses, but I never got close to anyone. I lied about myself to many of them. It was only when we were leaving school that I apologised to my friends and told them I don't live in a bungalow". In class nine, Hina had two good friends, Joanna and Uma, and together they were called 'HUJ'. The girls would stay back after school and concoct horror stories. Another good friend, Pranav Rasal, whom she met at a coaching centre in class ten and continues to be in touch with, said, "She's one of those people you can love or hate but cannot ignore. We started off as frenemies as we always competed for the number one position on tests, but over time we got to know each other well and became fast friends. She's honest and very strong-headed, but her intuition is quite strong, so usually she is right".

Innate Talent

Hina was extremely imaginative and would create interesting stories in her mind and often write them down. "Hina's love for creative writing seems to have been inherited from her paternal grandfather, who was a writer for films. She started writing when she was in class 4. I do not remember her reading any Mills and Boons or fairytales ever. She was instead interested in books based on fantasy fiction, history, biographies and the like. She was always well-informed about everything", said Poornima*ji*. What was unique in Hina's writing journey was that while she started very young, she wasn't writing poetry or stories but writing plays. "In primary school, I started writing X–Files fanfiction. In one of the episodes, I saw a man dying and his dead body being swarmed by cockroaches and I wrote a story around it. I made a binder of loose sheets to start writing my X–Files fan fiction and other stories", she said. However, the disturbing image from the series stayed with her, and she's scared of cockroaches even today. Hina also developed her own unique style of writing. "When people talk of playwriting, it's a structured form of writing and not free-flowing. I developed a template based on my instinctive form of writing".

Disturbances in Developmental Years

However, Hina's childhood was marred by a disturbing home environment. Her family was conservative in many ways. Her uncle and grandmother interfered in their family matters and exerted control, especially in matters involving the girls. She remembers one of these incidents:

> I was tall for my age group and was physically developing faster than other girls my age. In class six or seven, I disappeared for a whole day. I had gone to a friend's place. We ate a cake there. Her mom was also present. When I returned home, there was a huge hue and cry. My uncle assumed I was having an affair or being taken advantage of. My mom was asked to take me to the bathroom and check if I had any signs of something gone wrong. I don't think that the adults had any idea that I knew exactly what they were talking about. This kind of oppression

> towards us girls characterised those years. The repressive environment damaged Subuhi more than Hina, as she was not only seven years older than her sister, but also more feminine in her ways. Her parents' focus on her older sister left Hina with a feeling of neglect. "It took me a lot of time to process the need to be taken care of".

Hina didn't like the restrictive environment at home, and learning from her sister's example, she kept most of her personal problems to herself, tackling them on her own. "No one knew what I was doing in school...or boys teasing me on the road ...I never brought home my problems. I faced it all alone", she said. Hina also felt her father was to be blamed equally for the unfair treatment that both the girls received at home, but he had a liberal side too. "I can't say my father didn't play any part in all this...but I've seen the same father explaining menstruation to me. I haven't seen any other father do that", she said. She also added:

A lot of people in our neighbourhood were from the Kasai community. One of their wives would come home to help Mom with household chores. The woman was getting her sixteen-year-old daughter married. I remember my dad took a stand against that and gave her a sit-down lecture. Yet again, when it came to his daughters, he would become extremely harsh. He had that oppressive presence and was violent. It was more the effect of the environment than him as a person. Hina's father was also addicted to gambling and had a drinking problem, which further vitiated their home environment. "Almost all my life, my mother and my sister have handled the finances of the house. They've been the breadwinners...Violence became my dad's way of exerting control, and it really affected our worldview". Subuhi didn't get along with her mother as her mother rarely took her side. Consequently, she "lost faith in her mother figure", but she was protective of her younger sister even though they were not too close as children. Hina is quite attached to both her mother and her sister. "My mom and my sister are two of the strongest people I know. I admire them deeply", she said.

Hina completed her secondary schooling with satisfactory grades in 2002, and joined Nowrosjee Wadia College for Arts and Science for Junior college. It was there that Hina's journey as a Theatre artist was initiated.

RAY FLORET

(Youth)

Hina applied for her B.Sc. in the same college in 2005 after completing Junior College. "It was my dream to go abroad and study. I got admission in a university abroad but realised we couldn't afford to pay for it", she said. Hina gave up her dream of doing biotechnology, dropped out of college after her first year, went to a different college in her second year and then dropped out again. "There was nothing holding me to science. I wanted to be a genetic engineer because there was a passionate narrative around it, but I couldn't go abroad, so I dropped out". In 2007, Hina was admitted to Pune University to complete her B.A. through distance learning. "I was always interested in stories", said Hina, explaining why she changed her stream to Arts. "I loved learning about culture, religion, mythology, and folklore. I came across the word 'anthropology' and got interested. Pune University had a very good Anthropology department. I had no intention of doing my Bachelor's, but I took admission just because I wanted to study Anthropology. I actually enjoyed writing the papers". Hina had also started supporting herself financially by working part-time since Junior College. She worked with different companies, including as a waiter at Café Coffee Day, and a salesperson at Crossword Bookstore.

By this time, Subuhi, who'd started working with an MNC call centre, had bought a one BHK house in a better locality. Poornima*ji* decided to move into the new house with both her daughters, while Hina's grandmother and father continued to stay in the old house. "Subuhi was sent to the US for a training programme. She worked really hard to save up money in dollars, came back and bought a house", said Hina.

Hina often visited her grandmother, who was bedridden after experiencing a bad fall. "It was close to my college, and I went there for the hundred-rupee note I got every time I visited her. She doted on me because her grandson—whom she liked best among her grandchildren—had shifted abroad". After some time, Hina's father also moved into the new house to live with his wife and daughters. Her grandmother's health deteriorated, so she shifted in with the family. She eventually became bedridden and passed away in the new house.

Beginnings of Success

Hina had already shown her creative bent as a theatre artist by writing and directing a one-act play during her Junior College years. It became a huge hit and was shown as a standalone play in college many times. "It was here that I picked up the finer nuances of how to create theatre", she said. During this time, she met a few like-minded people who loved theatre just like her. One of them was her college friend, Prerna, who belonged to an affluent family. Over time, Prerna became a close friend, and after college, Hina would often spend time at her friend's house. "I was there at her house for every major event. I was also there for her marriage", she said. However, the first time Prerna confessed to being attracted to a guy, Hina felt a sense of betrayal. "I think our relationship stopped being what it was after that point. I was a horrible friend to her".

The success of her one-act play in college gave Hina a confidence boost and propelled her to explore theatre. Along with some of her friends, she joined a community theatre group. This was the only platform of its kind in the city in those days, and they often gave chances to amateur artists. In 2007, Hina wrote another one-act play, *Mind Matters*, and approached the theatre group to produce her play, but the founder refused her request. It was then that Hina—along with her friends, Irisha, Prerna, and Yazdi (one of the performers from the community theatre group)—joined hands, and thus Orchestrated Q'Works (OQ) was born. It was Hina's ambition to see the play she'd written see the light of day that propelled her to start her theatre group.

"My school friend, Chetna's mom, gave us five thousand rupees, and we arranged the rest of the money for the play ourselves", said Hina. Their first offering to the public eye were two one-act plays, her own play, *Mind Matters,* and *Bloody Mary*, a play she'd found online. Her own play was about the life of a psychiatrist and how she cured patients, with Hina playing the role of the psychiatrist. The play was well received, but it was also criticised for being insensitive towards the plight of those with mental health problems by a Parsi gentleman who happened to suffer from similar problems himself. Hina met up with the gentleman, understood his perspective and made changes to her play. "The humour in the play remained, but it became more humane", she said. The second one-act play, *Bloody Mary,* was a strange story of a girl shot in the stomach, seeking help from a maimed man.

Hina met her mentor and guide, Mahrukh Barucha—a well-known Theatre professional—while she was still in the process of starting her theatre group OQ. Mahrukh guided her on the technicalities of theatre-making. "Hina was a sprightly 23-year-old stranger who literally barged into my studio one evening all those years ago and announced, "I want to do theatre." We had a long conversation, mainly where I asked a few questions, and she responded with disarming candour and complete authenticity", said Mahrukh. "I was able to mentor her when she started OQ by guiding her focus to the organisational intricacies she tended to miss because she was so caught up with the creative work".

Shortly, after the success of her plays under OQ, Hina acted in a play directed by Mahrukh. She also started her formal drama training at Mahrukh's academy. After some time, she also began teaching Speech and Drama in Mahrukh's academy. "She has taught me far more than I could have ever taught her. My teaching has been conscious...her sharing of knowledge, skills and perspective are always spontaneously generous and hugely astute to recognize and refill any lacunae in my life at point in time", said Mahrukh. "Our relationship has evolved from a teacher-student dynamic to a wonderful state she terms as 'found family'". Hina continued to work in Mahrukh's Academy for the next three years.

Struggles with Identity

In her personal life, however, Hina felt disturbed and was continuously fighting her inner demons:

> I learnt about my queerness and asexuality only four or five years ago. However, it's this massive trauma I've carried within myself for a long time that no one is attracted to me. I've always wondered, what is wrong with me? Why doesn't anyone go out with me? Whenever I've had people date me, they never want a second date. Most people's idea of attraction, romance and interest is conflated. The idea of liking someone is attached to romantic undertones. I grew up with the same beliefs. Now, when I like someone, I say, "let's go out for coffee", but it doesn't need to have a romantic connotation. It's sometimes hard to figure out whether you actually want something or if you are conditioned to want something. The grief of letting go of this idea, that 'this can't be my life' affected me, and my self-worth took a massive beating. Most of us who use a specific word like 'queer' or 'neurodivergent' or 'asexual' or 'transgender' use these words after consistent misunderstanding and marginalisation from conventional society. We feel like outsiders, and we need words to describe this feeling of 'outsider-ness'.

Hina's need to be understood and appreciated compelled her to get into multiple toxic relationships, which further left her in anguish and with self-destructive behaviour. While she was an emotional wreck on the inside, she continued to write and direct plays on different, serious, and meaningful topics under OQ, with many of them winning recognition and appreciation.

In 2009, she was invited to the Women's International Playwright Conference held in Mumbai, which was a turning point for her. "This was the first time I tried to travel alone to Mumbai and had this massive showdown with my dad. I remember crying on the rickshaw on the way to the bus stop", she said. Hina, however, had a wonderful time at the conference as this was the first time she encountered "Queer people making art". It was also the first time she learnt about the different understanding of practices from around the world. Playwrights from across the world were present at the event. Hina said she was recognised for herself. "People saw me. I felt I belonged here. For the first time, I was surrounded by Queer people". She said, "The pressure of being surrounded by the male gaze or the heteronormative view wasn't there".

After this exposure, Hina said she also evolved as an artist and developed her theatrical language. When she returned to Pune, her group staged a performance based on a Canadian Playwright's play, *Sapphire Butterfly Blue*, which had been staged at the Mumbai conference and had positively impacted Hina. Unlike a linear play, this play was a "burst of scenes" and was about the need for people to blame others and finding creative ways to do it. Another important milestone moment was in 2010, when Hina and her team were planning to stage a play originally written by Sham Shepard titled *Geography of a Horse Dreamer.* Yazdi was to direct the play, but due to creative differences, he left the play midway and later withdrew from OQ. Hina went on to direct the play, which talked about the inner world and insecurities of the artistic mind through the metaphor of Cody, a young man who dreamt about which horses would win the race. The play was very well received. From here on, Hina became the sole owner of Orchestrated Q Works.

FULL BLOOM

(Present)

In 2011, Hina was invited to the UK for a two-week long "Contacting the World" programme. The international project was for a year, and the organisers selected six British and six non-British companies, who were paired and created productions together. While OQ didn't qualify, Hina was invited as a theatre-maker and founder of OQ at the end of the year to Manchester (UK). "Mahrukh helped me raise funds by appealing to the community in Pune", said Hina.

One of Hina's maternal uncles lives in London, so Hina divided her time in the UK by spending a week in Manchester, and then living with her uncle in London. It was an immersive experience for her. For the first time, she felt independent and comfortable surrounded by her kind of people. "It was, for me, the epitome of freedom. Every day I was watching plays and doing things I loved", she said. After returning from the UK, Hina's theatrical practice evolved, and it became increasingly visible in her work. She had been unconsciously applying the principles of Epic Theatre and Experimental Theatre in her work from the start, but it became more pronounced after her international exposure. "My chosen form of theatre is surreal, episodic; telling the tales of different people through different perspectives, and very symbolic", she said. "This was a point of disagreement between Yazdi and me. Linearity is not my thing. Creating chaos has been my classical language".

Grappling with Depression

In the same year, Hina joined her first full-time job at a well-known convent school in the city as a Drama teacher. She was twenty-three and had already seen some success as a theatre artist and founder of a theatre group. "I was making a lot of plays about abuse, child abuse, sexual violence, female foeticide, insanity, etcetera".

After she got a full-time job, Hina moved out of her sister's house to live on her own. She loved having her own independent space and lived in the rented house for a year. However, on the work front, the structured environment of the school started affecting her. "You weren't allowed to be yourself. You were supposed to dress up in a certain way, speak a certain way, submit regular reports...Moreover, I was the only single woman, the rest were married, so I had little to contribute to their conversation", she said. "Theatre became my way of exercising my emotional neediness", she reveals. "I moved to my second house, but it was one of the worst moves. It was dirty, and I couldn't bring myself to even go to the bathroom the first day".

The school environment, coupled with her shift to a new house, left her feeling disturbed. She went into a deep depression, and self-harm became her way of negatively coping with her emotional distress. She would cut herself at places that could be hidden by clothing. Often, she would go to sleep in the same condition, and at times, she even went to school in that state. "I would hold a pin in my hand and teach". Mahrukh noticed the wounds on her hand and showed concern. She tried to have a conversation with Hina about the issue, but it didn't help.

Hina's depression was so horrific that after a point, Mahrukh had to step back as Hina would ignore her phone calls and not show up for her theatre work either. This continued for a few years. It even affected her performance in school, and after three years of being a full-time teacher, she started teaching only part-time. The school had three wings, and only the Principal of the secondary wing was fine to let her continue with them. Because of this, Hina moved back in with her parents. By then, Subuhi had gotten married, and her first house had been sold off to pay for the Daycare Centre she wanted to start. Her parents moved to a 2 BHK rented house, where Hina was given her own room. However, her volatile emotional state overwhelmed her, and she often called in sick at school. Her parents were confused and didn't know how to deal with her emotional turmoil. "They had no clue what or who I was".

Self-harm became Hina's way of externalising her pain and feeling better. "Everyone was like, there's nothing wrong with your life, so what are you depressed about? I was just overwhelmed with everything", she said. "I didn't feel like I belonged in any space. There is only so much alienation you can deal with. I am saying words, but no one understands. I'm asking for attention, but no one is giving it to me". Her childhood practice of imagining things skyrocketed at this point, and caused her much disappointment and pain in her intimate relationships. She said it happened to her several times that she found herself in an intimate relationship, with no acknowledgement of the relationship. "I think in the heteronormative world, everything is assumed. There is no clarity".

This was also the time when Hina wrote and directed one of her most critically acclaimed plays, *White Noise. She was* influenced by William Dalrymple's book, *Nine Lives. Her*

distinctive style involving episodic plot structure, narrating poignant stories of different people was extremely well received in Pune. However, a certain section of political people in the audience objected to certain elements of the play when it was first presented. "We darkened the stage and eased the content", she said. The play travelled to Mumbai's Kala Ghoda Festival (2012), Delhi's Fourth Terrace Theatre Festival (2012) and Kolkata. "This was a play that caught the eyes of people".

Finding her Bearings

Hina was around twenty-seven when a serious road accident left her bedridden for six months. The accident also changed the course of her personal and artistic journey. It was the height of summer, and Hina was returning from school in her scooter. She was travelling at high speed when she spotted a cat trying to cross the road. By the time she applied the brakes, it was already too late, and Hina hit the cat. The scooter skidded for another twenty feet with her legs caught between the scooter and the ground, and her left knee was completely uprooted. Despite the seriousness of her accident, she had the presence of mind to call her mom. Hina was admitted to the hospital for a week and, after a major surgery, she was put on bed rest for six months. It was during this time that she started processing how her life had been so far and whether she'd have a say in how it shapes up in the future. "After my recovery, I realised I needed control over my life. I can't lose it all the time".

In 2013, immediately after her recovery, Hina conducted a theatre workshop titled "Girls! Get on Stage!", and it was the first of its kind in Pune. It was also the point at which her life took a different turn. A longtime friend, Sanam Gandhi, who is an artist, actor, and activist—and one of the first transwomen who got her name and gender changed on official documents as per the new laws—recalled how she read about Hina's theatre workshop for the first time. "The newspaper notice mentioned that the workshop was for everyone who identified as a woman. I called her up and told her, "I was born as a male, but I know I'm a female. Can I join your workshop?" Hina lovingly welcomed me not only to the workshop but also in her life". During this time, Hina was also exploring other opportunities and decided to call Jehan Manekshaw, the erstwhile Head of Drama School Mumbai (DSM), whom she'd met earlier. The meeting went well, though nothing immediate came of it. She returned to Pune and began working with a couple of restaurants and Cafes, procuring artists and curating their afternoon programmes. She also organised a Theatre Festival, which received a lukewarm response, although her play on hook-up culture opened to a full house.

In 2016, Hina joined DSM as their Communications Head, and it became her main source of income. She worked with them till 2020. During this time, her name was recommended for a prestigious fellowship programme called ATSA. Under the fellowship, Hina completed the two-week training in Delhi and then travelled to the UK for her secondment in 2017. She also got an opportunity to intern briefly at the Spill International Festival, UK. Around this time, Hina moved out of her parent's house again, as her sister, who was separated from her husband, came back. "I shifted as it again became a chaotic atmosphere", she said. Hina was still directing plays under OQ, but slowly, her attention shifted to theatre-making, a process of creating new ensembles and immersive pieces through long-term collaborative experimentation.

Her play, *Coming Out*, which was performed in 2016-17, was about moments of non-conformity and queerness. On the opening night of the show, people turned up in large numbers, and the group did a second impromptu show to accommodate them all.

In her intimate relationships, until this point, the people Hina was attracted to were still men. "For the longest time in my life, I've wanted to talk about who I am, but nobody listened. My queerness is different. I'm attracted to everyone but not sexually. I just want to be close to people and hug them. I'm gender-fluid. I gave attention to these aspects and started articulating who I am for myself and then to others in 2020 and 2021", she said.

In 2019, Hina left DSM and joined Gyaan Adab, a well-known and celebrated literary and cultural centre in Pune. She joined them as their Programme Head and worked till the pandemic lockdown forced the centre to shut down. "During lockdown, I wrote a play with stories in my head. It was called '*2D Crush*' and was about the alienation I felt due to the Covid lockdown," she said. "That play was where it started. Before that, I was processing my childhood trauma, and by 2020, I was done with it. My plays had been full of depressive and dark notes. I was processing a lot of my angst in my plays", she said. The pandemic changed her focus.

Major Career Transitions

In 2021, Hina joined a gaming company:

> Introducing her work (on her website), she wrote, "In order to keep the hearth burning, I started writing for a gaming company and came across the word 'transmedia' while studying narrative design. It was one of those moments, where something one resists all their life suddenly becomes the most obvious kind of truth. Video games made me realise that stories need not be constrained by form, graphics, or words; that there is power in the thought, "Why do it one way when you can do it all ways!

However, the job was hectic and had a toxic work environment. Hina's colleagues who worked under her weren't told that she was the Creative Producer of the project. They were unhappy with the work environment but kept silent. The leader of the team triggered the members to give negative feedback about her work. "This was not malicious at their end. I was not a victim of office bullying, but I was the only one who couldn't adapt to their toxic culture of blame-mongering and appeasement. The workload was immense, and there was a general lack of sensitivity", she said. Hina was also masking her neurodivergence at work. "It was clear that people like me would not be accepted", she said. Her health kept deteriorating, and her blood sugar levels spiked over 400 mg/dl. She also came down with dengue. Once Hina submitted her papers and was serving her notice period, her father had to be admitted to the hospital for a heart operation. She went to see him but was admitted to the same hospital because of her alarming health condition. Once she recovered physically, she shifted to her sister's house and started rebuilding her life slowly.

"At the end of 2021, while working on constant crunch in a queerphobic environment, I had a complete physical and mental breakdown that landed me in the ICU. This time, for the first time ever, I allowed myself to truly embrace the helplessness of my situation. I allowed my body, heart and mind to put down the burden of living in a world not designed for people like me", she said. "It was like I was starting my adult life again at the age of 36. But this time off from work allowed me to take care of my mother when she had a severe fall. It allowed me to start researching people—queer, autistic, aro-ace, genderqueer, non-normative people in their 50s and 60s—who could be role models for me. It also gave me a chance to start interacting with people, who were often much younger than me, and were building a kinder, more inclusive future through gaming.

Community and Strength

In 2021, Hina decided to informally adopt four or five children. Her adopted children are all adults, well into their twenties, and one even in his early thirties. "During the Pandemic, there was a collective decision among a few of us to become family to one another. The idea is to share the responsibility, the nurturing, the caregiving, the caretaking in this space", she said. Luv Mahatani, her first adopted child, who has known her since 2014 when he was still in college and attended one of her performances, said he found her "fun, entertaining and eccentric". He said he knew immediately that she was the kind of person he wanted to be friends with. "She looks at her close friends as her chosen family, and I love that concept. She has adopted a bunch of younglings from her friend circle and calls them her children. I'm one of them. I credit her for helping me shape my understanding of the creative world", said Luv.

After Hina quit her job at the gaming company, she joined a three-month course to learn game-making. This course was especially for marginalized communities interested in gaming.

She also participated in several gaming jams and started interacting with game-makers and founders of gaming companies to understand the intricacies of the industry. Hina correspondingly shifted her focus from theatre to Transmedia Storytelling and Narrative Design. "My ultimate goal is to develop a community-driven transmedia studio that tells the stories of people on the margins".

Hina expressed her present outlook towards life beautifully:

> My life has been a lot of love and care, not just angst and weirdness. A very big thing about me is loving people, albeit in platonic ways, taking care of them, and holding space for them. This radiates from my chosen family to almost everyone I cross paths with. However, I'm finally at a place where I don't equate my work with my identity. I am a person still struggling to figure out who I am while simultaneously being utterly sure of who I am. For the most part, I suppose, I am the space that I have always wanted to belong to, if that makes sense...a space that is kind and slow, a space where I can rest and create, tell stories, and let stories unfold and be told. A place where there is affection and intimacy, and the potential to build family beyond the constraints of birth and romance.

4

Kanika Dhillon

Author, Screenwriter and Producer

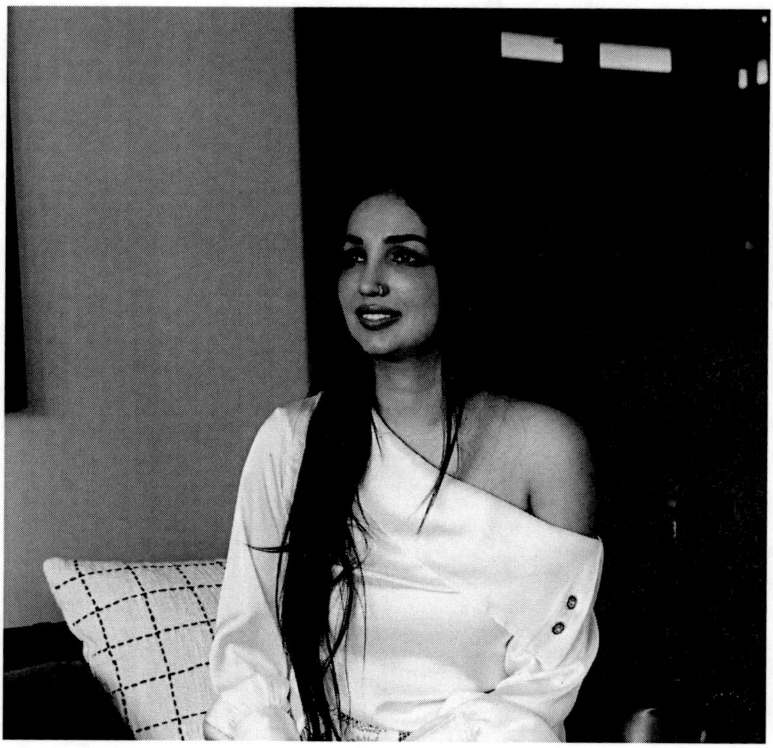

Figure 4

"Comfort can kill dreams...Very early in my life, I'd learnt not to get too comfortable if I wanted to pursue my passion."

—Kanika Dhillon

KANIKA DHILLON (b. 1984) is an author, screenwriter, and producer, holding a firm belief in the power of storytelling. Not only has she harnessed this power in the written word through her three acclaimed novels—*Bombay Duck is a Fish* (2011), *Shiva and the Rise of the Shadows* (2013), and *The Dance of Durga* (2016)—but also through the visual grammar of cinema, both as a writer and producer. The diversity in the genres and characters she creates for films results from her desire to achieve a distinct freshness in entertainment and communication with dynamic audiences. Known for curating strong female narratives through films and characters such as Rumi from *Mannmarziyaan*, Mukku from *Kedarnath*, Nani from *Guilty*, Bobby from *Judgemental Hai Kya*, and Rani from *Haseen Dillruba* amongst others, Kanika has always aimed at shaping her women as how they are in reality: raw, rooted, fiery and vulnerable all at once. Having collaborated with several highly regarded artists from the film industry, her vision for the future is filled with optimism and an enthused spirit to expand the boundaries of Indian Cinema. In 2012, Kanika was recognized as being among the "Top 30 under 30" by Hindustan Times at their annual youth summit. She also won the Best Dialogue award for the film *Haseen Dillruba* by OTTplay Awards 2022. In 2022, two of her films, *Haseen Dillruba* and *Rashmi Rocket,* also won multiple nominations at the prestigious 67th Filmfare Awards for their quirky and empowering women-led stories.

STARBUD

(Childhood)

Kanika was born in her ancestral home in Khankot in Amritsar, Punjab. Her father, H.S. Dhillon, was a businessman and owned rice mills, and her mother, Sunita Dhillon, was a professor in one of the most prominent women's colleges in Amritsar, and later retired as its principal. Kanika's childhood was raw, fun, and filled with mindless, crazy activities such as running alongside the trains passing through their village and taking rice baths with her elder sister, Harman, as white rice would spout out from a rice milling machine. "We were rowdy kids and were often up to some mischief", said Kanika. In fact, while writing her novel *Dance of Durga,* she explored her childhood memories of Khankot along with "heavy reflections" of her village.

Her sister, Harman, revealed how the two of them were often dressed up in similar outfits by their mother. "We put up a mean dance performance together once in a while", Harman added. "Kanika, however, is the one who is the dancer and used to choreograph the sequences. I barely managed to keep up. We called ourselves the 'Khankot sisters'".

The sisters also have a younger brother, who is six years younger than Kanika. When he was still an infant, Kanika liked to babysit him and play with him, but it was her elder sister who shared a great bond with her due to their closeness in age. The family's favourite pastime was watching cricket and films, and they "watched a lot of them". Kanika's mother, Sunita*ji,* described her daughter as "affectionate, curious, observant, and fun-loving" as a child. While village life was idle, Kanika loved reading stories and was always surrounded by them. "She showed her passion for storytelling from a very young age. I recall, she was about four or five years old and would wear my heels, and drape my dupatta as a saree, and make our gardener, our washerwoman, her kids and our cook sit in the verandah and tell them "I'm going to tell you a story" and then proceed to read out and somewhat enact a story from her English reader", her mother disclosed.

Kanika's love for books was so deep that she would read stories even in poor lighting. Her mother, she said, would lock the books in a cupboard before leaving for college.

Kanika started her schooling with her sister in DAV Public School, Amritsar, when her parents shifted to the city in the early 90s. She was enrolled in class one, and while she loved reading story books, she didn't take much of a liking to school books. Weekends and holidays were still spent in their village farmhouse along with the family.

Political Turmoil and Discovering a Love for Films

The insurgency in Punjab from the mid-1980s to the mid-1990s impacted Kanika's young mind greatly. She said she was quite small and didn't quite fully understand what was happening, but she could sense things. "Emotionally it was quite a difficult period", she said. She saw many of her father's friends come and stay in their house. Life went on as usual for the children, but the evening curfew alarm was disturbing, confusing and even frightening. "I remember a friend's father was shot point blank", said Kanika. The news had a distressing effect on her. It was becoming difficult to stay on the farm, so the entire family (including her grandparents) shifted to Amritsar. Only her father would visit the village to oversee their farmland occasionally.

Kanika was around twelve when the insurgency came to an end. "The first film we went to watch in a theatre as a family—without the fear of feeling being bombed—was *Hum Aapke Hain Kaun*". Kanika said the movie outing experience with her family after a long period of forced confinement gave her a sense of freedom, and it was then that the urge to be a part of the cinema came to her. "Going to a film theatre with the family was like a celebration". The fact that cinema had such an impact on people and brought joy to them fascinated her. "I associated going to the theatre as something joyous. Books, I already enjoyed, and theatre too, after all, was just storytelling".

Figuring out her Priorities

Despite her love for books, Kanika had no interest in studies till middle-school and often bunked her classes. However, her sister Harman was a bright student and did well throughout her academic life. Kanika was known for being a great dancer. Along with her close friends, Neeti, Shruti, and Anchal, she would often represent her school at dance competitions and win. In fact, dance practice became an excuse for the girls to bunk classes. Around the same time, Kanika flunked her math exam. This came as a huge shock and embarrassment to her, and jolted her out of her stupor and careless attitude towards her studies. There was a retest and she scored 99/100 in the subject. After this incident, she said she started taking her studies seriously and "aced" all subjects. Her childhood friend, Neeti, who has known her since they were in class four, said, "Kanika was an all-rounder...be it dance competitions, declamations, debates, or academics. She was a favourite among teachers and was even chosen as the head girl of the school". She also described her friend as being "jovial, lively and naughty". Another of her childhood friends, Shivpriya, said that Kanika is not only a strong person but always knew what she wanted and pursued it.

RAY FLORET

(Youth)

After completing her schooling in 2001 with top scores in all subjects, Kanika got admission to St. Stephens College, Delhi. She excelled in college too. Even before Kanika had completed her senior secondary education, she'd disclosed to her parents that she wanted to pursue writing seriously. However, writing wasn't considered a profession then, and her parents were keen that their younger daughter complete her senior secondary education and try for either an MBA or IAS. Kanika said that between the two options, she decided to choose IAS as it would give her ample time to write. "I didn't share these devious plans with my family", she revealed.

However, destiny had other plans for her. In her final year of college, she applied for a master's degree at the London School of Economics (LSE) and secured admission. After graduating in 2004, she took an interim break to prepare for LSE. During this period, she completed a diploma course in marketing and advertising from St. Xaviers. Kanika was twenty-three when she got her master's degree from LSE in 2006. Her time in London, she said, was a blur as she had no free time. She was busy with her studies and juggling three jobs, as she didn't want her parents to pay. However, the people around her, especially the Indian community, were very supportive and helped her in various ways.

Fighting all Odds for Passion

After finishing her master's degree, Kanika received a job offer from LSE with a good pay package, and her family was thrilled. While everyone around her was happy, Kanika felt restless. "I had palpitations because I thought I'll get comfortable with a job which would earn me good money...it was a big achievement, but I knew I would be miserable", she said. So, Kanika lied to her parents and told them she had to prepare her dissertation, for which she needed to travel to Mumbai. Her sister, Harman, helped her in a big way and called her friends to ensure Kanika had a place to stay in Mumbai.

Kanika took an extension from her workplace (LSE) and landed in Mumbai with no concrete plans (or connections); all she knew was that she had to give herself a chance and see if she could realise her dream. She randomly called up many people, and among them was Bobby Chawla, the CEO of Shahrukh Khan's production house, Red Chillies Entertainment, at the time. He informed her that she was overqualified for the job of an intern. She still went ahead and met him and got the job.

Kanika returned to London, submitted her dissertation, and then told her parents she was joining Shah Rukh Khan's production house in Mumbai. Her parents thought their daughter was too tired of studying and was taking a break, but that she would soon come to her senses. By that time, her sister Harman had also shifted to Mumbai, which came as a huge relief for Kanika, as she not only had a place to stay but also had the immediate support of her strongest ally. She knew she wouldn't leave Mumbai without giving her best shot to fulfil her goal of becoming a writer. Her mother, Sunita*ji*, said, "Both my husband and I were clear that we shall not impose our choices and perspective onto our children, hence, we did not oppose Kanika when she decided to work for the Indian Film Industry".

About the nature of her job during her initial days at Red Chillies, Kanika said she was everybody's assistant and was doing all sorts of work. "This industry is very chaotic. There's no entry point. I knew I had to self-teach myself. I decided I won't say no to anything. Everything was a learning experience. I had no one to guide me, the only famous writers I knew were Salim and Javed and, of course, I could not ask them to mentor me. I had snippets of work and got to learn a lot during my time in Red Chillies". She also said that most of her learning came from being a director's assistant (AD), especially about what not to do. She took a keen interest in reading the scripts and memorized them, be it ad films or feature films, and a lot of her learning happened by observing Farah Khan, Shah Rukh Khan, and others.

Since she was self-learning, there was a lot of anxiety too, she said. "Everybody was there with a dream and an ambition, and everyone knew that only a handful can make it. I fought my doubts everyday, but you cannot wallow in self-pity. You can be replaced in hours". *Ra. One* was the first film she was fully a part of, and what delighted her the most was seeing her name in the credits of the film. She said that being a part of that film was also a big learning curve for her. Despite her hard work and dedication, she had to face several challenges, including gender bias. Kanika said:

> Initially, people felt they could easily dismiss me, and they always ended up being surprised. The first director I got a chance to work with was Farah Khan. Somehow, I had this knack for standing at the wrong place at the wrong time during the shootings. Later, I found out that everybody had placed a bet on how long I'd survive—forget the film industry—on the sets. Some said five days, while others said a month at most. But hello, here I am!

Kanika wrote her first novel, *Bombay Duck is a Fish*, in 2011, while juggling multiple jobs at Red Chillies. The book was launched by Shah Rukh Khan. She said she felt overwhelmed by his kind gesture. "It was as if I was in seventh heaven". However, Kanika's joys were short-lived. When the reviews for the book started pouring in, one of the top writers Kanika admired gave a bad review and said she shouldn't write. "I used to look up to her, and here this person was telling me to never write. I was hugely shattered". After the initial disappointment wore off, Kanika self-reflected and came to the conclusion that other people's opinions of her work would not decide what would happen to her career. The power to decide her life choices would always reside with her. She decided to take a break for a couple of years, and did a short stint with Ekta Kapoor, curating content for Balaji Telefilms in 2012. During this time, she also wrote her second novel, *Shiva and the Rise of the Shadows*. Her work with Ekta Kapoor was fetching her good money and was also being appreciated, but she said her heart was always in creating content and not curating it. She left Balaji Telefilms in 2013. This was also the time when she started writing the script for *Manmarziyaan*.

Falling into Place

Kanika recalls her time at Balaji with fondness. She said her first brush with them was many years ago, when they held a writing contest for TV. She'd participated in the contest and was one of the five winners. They were offering selected writers boarding and lodging and a writing fee too. It was a great exercise, she said, adding that others in the industry should emulate them, but Kanika did not join them as she wanted to write for films. "I knew that writing for TV is different from writing for movies and it would be difficult to make the switch once I started writing for TV".

Even after working with well-known production houses like Red Chillies and Balaji Telefilms, and being a published author, Kanika continued to face difficulties in establishing herself as a writer in the film industry. After leaving Balaji, she completed the script of *Manmarziyaan*. The journey of *Manmarziyaan* was also quite painful, with major changes in all aspects of filming. It got cast and then re-casted. It even got shelved. There was a time when Kanika even felt that the movie would never be made. She started doubting her own decisions regarding the film.

It was only after Anurag Kashyap decided to direct the film that she realised that all her decisions were right. "If you're not tasting success, it's very easy to kind of regret your choices", she said. However, *Manmarziyaan* was also the film that introduced her to her future husband, Himanshu Sharma. She met him in 2016, when she went to narrate the script to producer Aanand L. Rai, and Himanshu, who was also one of the co-producers of the film, was at the meeting too. "I was absolutely into the script...I felt it was a new voice and this opinion continues. It's my favourite film of hers", Himanshu said. The two started dating each other in 2017. Himanshu said that while he's laid back and a lazy guy, Kanika is dedicated, passionate and great at multitasking. He admires his wife for her dedication towards all areas of her life, be it her work, writing, tending to their infant son Veer, or managing the house. "There's so much to learn from her", he said.

FULL BLOOM

(Present)

Manmarziyaan was released in 2018 and was well-received at the box office. It earned her some much-deserved name and fame. Yet, the film got in trouble, and Kanika had her first brush with controversy. In one scene, the female lead remembers her lover while getting married, which upset certain audiences. In one of her interviews to Komal Sinha of *Talepost media*, Kanika spoke her mind and said she writes modern-day love stories and wants to create characters that are "as genuine and as raw as possible". In the same interview, she even called the writing of the film a "liberating experience". After *Manmarziyaan,* there was no looking back. That same year, *Kedarnath* was released, and it further cemented her position as a scriptwriter. Kanika has been called a highly provocative writer by author and film critic Anupama Chopra.

Most of Kanika's women characters are raw, outspoken, and unapologetic and show her own feminist beliefs. Over the years, she has been entangled in several controversies because of her portrayal of bold and whacky female characters in her stories, and has been strongly rebutting the thought systems that are different from hers. In one of their articles, India Today described her as "authentic, candid and defiant". Her husband, Himanshu, has high praise for his wife, saying, "her female characters are brave and amazing. They're flawed. They're not perfect people". He also said that his wife has used her education well, along with her creative streak. Moreover, she's aware of her capabilities and voices her opinion. She's not only focused and meticulous with her research but also understands the commerce side of the business, he said. A similar view was expressed by Kanika's good friend, Taapsee Pannu, who has also been the female lead in many of the films for which Kanika has written the script. "What I admire about Kanika is her ability to adapt to circumstances. She makes the most of every opportunity that she wants to seize", she said.

Finding Light in Dark Times

Kanika was writing her third book, *The Dance of Durga*, when she suffered a huge personal loss. She lost her father suddenly due to a massive heart attack. A night before his passing, he'd called her several times, but she'd been unable to take his calls. This left her feeling emotionally distressed and unstable for a long time. This phase between 2016 and 2018 was an extremely painful period for Kanika and her family, and she had a mental breakdown as well.

She couldn't get on a flight for two years as it would make her severely anxious. She avoided crowded places altogether and had to take anti-anxiety medication. She was even admitted to a hospital but tried to jump out of its window. She had to be given injections to calm down. Her family was around, but no one could help her, she said. The seed idea for the movie *Judgemental Hai Kya* was triggered by this personal tragedy. Her biggest setback was that she completely stopped writing due to the strong medicines, and this tormented her. She decided to stop the medication and instead took a shot of vodka whenever she had to take a flight, and strangely, it worked for her. She also turned to yoga and meditation to calm herself down. "I meditate till date", she disclosed.

Kanika also started reading a lot of self-help books and looking for ways to come out of her low phase. "I did not want to take medicines. It may not be correct. One must seek medical help. All the doctors I consulted were good to me", she said. However, she always carried the prescribed emergency medicines, in case she needed immediate attention. It took her six months after she stopped medicines to make a turnaround. Her son's presence and writing her book *Dance of Durga* really helped her, she said. The novel was released in 2016. Set in rural Punjab, the story was praised for the portrayal of its lead protagonist, Rajjo, who like Kanika's previous heroines, was depicted as quirky and flawed; and yet readers were drawn to her character.

Describing her daughter, Sunita*ji* said, "I think Kanika's greatest strength, if I may call it that, is her ability to be interested in other people and have empathy for their viewpoint, their dreams, their drawbacks and their idiosyncrasies. She has always been a keen observer and very mature in her analysis of any situation or reaction. All this was instrumental in churning out a gripping tale".

Recently, Kanika has also turned into a film producer. "Producing a film is a challenge. I'm looking forward to it... but writing will be a constant", she said.

Kanika Dhillon's own life journey from a young girl who loved reading books and telling stories, to becoming a celebrated Bollywood scriptwriter and producer is no less than a script for a Bollywood film. She continues to write and unapologetically explore the unexplored shades of a woman through her characters. As Taapsee puts it, "She doesn't believe in being the most righteous person and would rather be a normal human being who grows with each mistake she makes and takes it all in her stride, and doesn't get bogged down by it".

5

Manjot Kaur

Visual Artist

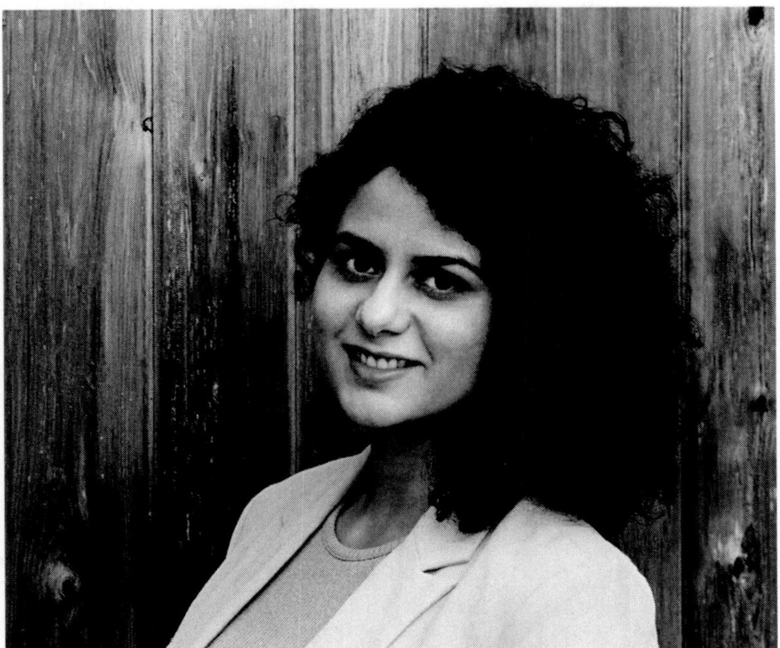

Figure 5

"I'm interested in creating new visual stories by cross-pollinating ancient motifs & attributes. Inventing fiction from mythology and to de-patrichize the existing dualist constructs of nature and culture, I want to propose narratives that imagine a multi-species future."

—Manjot Kaur

Manjot Kaur (b. 1989) is an accomplished visual artist with global recognition. She was a Visiting Artist Fellow at The Lakshmi Mittal and Family South Asia Institute at Harvard University, USA, from March to April 2023. She completed her B.F.A and M.F.A in Painting from Government College of Art, Panjab University, Chandigarh, in 2010 and 2012, respectively.

Introducing her work on her website, Manjot describes her drawings, paintings, and time-based media as an attempt to decolonise both women's bodies and the sovereignty of ecology. Her works explore the interconnection between humans and non-humans. Her detailed and intimate paintings invite viewers to ponder the symbiosis between humankind and ecology. How do the worlds we create in fantasies impact our present-day thinking practices? What are the consequences of fertility and the urge to procreate for the human species? How do we mourn what we have lost, and what efforts are required to regain the biodiversity that's currently on the verge of extinction? How to create a sustainable and respectable correlation between biodiversity and human progress to future-proof our planet for generations to come? How might this notion of non-sentient things like rivers and forests having rights be pushed further? These are some of the questions she tries to respond to through her paintings using her unique style. Increasingly, her works focus and reflect on the dependence and well-being of interspecies.

Manjot has been an artist-in-residence at Jan van Eyck Academie, Maastricht, Netherlands (2020-21), 1 Shanthiroad, Bangalore (2019), Unidee, Cittadellarte Fondazione Pistoletto, Italy (2018), supported by Inlaks Shivdasani Foundation, India and Peers-Khoj International Artists' Association, New Delhi (2018). Her recent participation includes "Becoming Earths" Gallery Caroline O'Brien, Amsterdam during Amsterdam Art Week (2023), India Art Fair, Gallery Latitude 28, New Delhi (2023), "Futur Proche", Apre Art House, Mumbai (2023), "Where Shall We Plant The Placenta", A Tale of A Tub, Rotterdam (2022), "Non-Fungible Speculations", Nature Morte, New Delhi (2022); "The World Awaits You Like a Garden", Latitude 28, New Delhi (2022), "The Pool of Memories", Surrey Art Gallery, Canada (2022), "Hurting and Healing—Let's Imagine a Different Heritage", Tensta Konsthall, Stockholm (2022), "Terrain Offline", Bikaner House, New Delhi, (2021), and "Garden State", Garage Rotterdam, Rotterdam, Netherlands (2021) among others. She has also received a Generator Art Production Fund from Experimenter Gallery, Kolkata (2022).

STAR BUD

(Childhood)

Manjot was born in a middle-class family in Ludhiana, one of the largest cities in the state of Punjab. Her father, (late) Jaspal Singh, had a government job, while her mother, Ant Kumari is a homemaker. Being an expert needlewoman and embroiderer, she would impart sewing classes to girls, and ran a boutique from her home. Manjot's earliest memories from childhood are of playing with her mother and elder brother, Kuldeep (who is four and a half years older than her), in their front courtyard and watching her mother sew.

Ant*ji* described Manjot as a beautiful and happy child. "She was like a doll. I used to stitch her clothes myself". Kuldeep—an acclaimed painter, Odissi dancer, and a Professor of Visual Arts at the University of Washington—described his sister as fun, easygoing and an extrovert; a '*mast-maula*' child. Manjot also described herself as a 'jolly' child who had many friends and loved to play outdoors, unlike her brother, who was more into drawing and painting from the very beginning.

As the primary caregiver, Ant*ji* was deeply involved in her kids' overall development. Their father was mostly away for work, and even when he was home, he liked to be on his own for the most part. However, in the winter, Jaspal*ji* would call both his children and play 'sitting games' with them, which they enjoyed. Yet, it was their mother the two would turn to most of the time, especially for fun outdoor games. Both parents, however, never discriminated between their children. "I treated both my children the same way. I wanted to bring them up equally. So did my husband", said Ant*ji*.

Manjot's brother was her first inspiration and guide. "We used to fight as siblings do. I used to watch him paint. Sometimes he would scold me and tell me to go away and not bother him… that would hurt me, but we were just kids", she said. "I would go back again after some time and silently look at what he was doing and how he was doing it". She not only watched Kuldeep paint but soon started copying him, sitting for hours to make her paintings perfect, like her brother's.

Manjot was admitted to Gujaranwala Guru Nanak Public School when she turned four. Kuldeep had also been admitted to the same school earlier and was already performing well. From a young age, Manjot was a keen observer. She was exceptionally good at minute detailing in her drawing. She would draw out a hand on paper and make fine and intricate Henna designs with a ballpoint pen on it, her mother revealed. She said she would often marvel at her daughter's talent and carefully save those designs and her other paintings under a mattress.

Developing her Genius

In her elementary years, Manjot loved reading storybooks. She regularly spent three to four hours digging into her books after finishing her school homework. She was more into outdoor activities and her friends. In class six, she was shifted to the senior branch of her school. Her brother, by then, had already made a name for himself and was a topper, also winning art competitions. He was also appointed the school vice-captain. "I was constantly compared to him in my studies and my behaviour", said Manjot. "At times, I would get upset at others, or I wouldn't bother at all. I even thought it was good for me, as he had made grounds for me to grow and nourish".

Manjot was above average in studies and loved science and math. “I enjoyed science a lot. Our science teacher, Kiranjeet Kaur, taught us with care...Now, whenever I go back to Ludhiana, I meet her sometimes. During the Covid lockdown, she asked me if I could give her art lessons. Our relationship has changed; she’s happy to see my progress”, she said.

By class eight, Manjot was sure that she wanted to be an artist and slowly started spending more time practising her art. “I was not a topper but was scoring consistently in the 80s. I was happy with that. I really, really loved the outdoors and would quickly finish my homework so that I could go and play outside”, she said. However, her interest in reading continued. She liked reading fiction, especially *Harry Potter*, *Goosebumps*, and other mystery books. “My brother was also a voracious reader and would buy this art series called *The Great Artists*”, she disclosed. “These were thin books about painters starting from the Renaissance period. They had biographies of artists with a lot of visuals. I would skim through the books”.

To devote more time to perfecting her art, Manjot decided to take up Humanities in class eleven. “When it comes to painting, I work in minute details and paint slow and precisely, so I realised that I needed to choose a stream which wouldn’t require a lot of my time”, she said. It was while pursuing Humanities that she started enjoying political science a lot. “Even now, when I study ‘Systems of Governance’ it excites me and has also become a part of my work. My interest in science and the politics of the natural world grew with time. It’s a mix of these subjects I studied in school that have resurfaced in my work”.

In class twelve, Manjot became the school’s vice-captain, just like her brother. Her art teacher involved Manjot in the school hallways’, decoration and other similar work. “My art teacher would say, “you cannot do everything. You have to focus”. I realized I was happier in my world of fine arts. I used to go to many art competitions, and that’s where I was winning all the prizes”. Kuldeep said the two were quite popular in school and were called the “art siblings of the school”. Manjot had many friends in school. One of her good friends, Jaspreet, was excellent at debate and declamations but wanting in art, so they both taught each other the skills they had. "We complimented and helped each other, and spent a lot of time together even after school", said Manjot. The two friends had to part ways when Jaspreet shifted to Canada for higher studies. "I was happy for her, but I had no such ambition. My aim was to go to a fine arts college in India". Manjot cleared her senior secondary in 2006 with good grades.

RAY FLORET

(Youth)

After passing out of school, Manjot applied to only two Art colleges: The Govt. College of Art, Panjab University, Chandigarh, and the Delhi College of Art, Delhi University, New Delhi. She successfully cleared the entrance exams for both. However, her experience in Delhi wasn't satisfactory. She fell ill and took her exam while running a high fever. She ranked 6th at Delhi College of Art and 16th at Government College of Art, Panjab University.

She decided to travel to both cities to look at the respective college campuses. She found Delhi less conducive to her health, given that she had bronchitis since childhood. "I realised it was a matter of clean air. Later in my life, I worked around these issues. The water we drink, the food we eat and the air we breathe became of prime importance for me…they touch me because of my personal health experiences", she said. Delhi College of Art also didn't offer hostel facilities to its students. Her brother was already in the same college and was struggling in Delhi. Moreover, it was Manjot's childhood dream to live in Chandigarh because it was a "clean and pretty city". "My Masi lived in Chandigarh. We would visit her during vacations. My brother, my cousin and I are the same age and would hang out together during those visits, and whenever I was in that city, I would imagine myself living there", she said. "So, when the chance came, I didn't think about the professional set-up or if the artistic opportunities such as galleries are more numerous in Delhi. I just thought I would live and study in Chandigarh".

An Idyllic Time

Manjot happily took admission into the college of her choice in 2006. She chose painting out of the four forms offered by the college under Fine Arts. Her hostel was just a kilometre away from the college. "I just couldn't wait to start there", she said. Each student was allotted a single room. "We didn't have to share rooms. You had your privacy". Manjot enjoyed her hostel life. For the first time, she was living away from home and doing things independently. Moreover, she found like-minded friends. The new joinees formed a group and would stick together. Since the college was close by, they would often walk to college, or at times, take a rickshaw. Unfortunately, the mess food was basic and barely palatable. Manjot recounted how her parents once visited her and insisted on having lunch with her at the mess, but gave up the idea as soon as they tried it.

The first year was a foundation year, and practical lessons were held during the day while they had their theory classes in the evenings. Students learning sculpture, painting, design, and print-making were shuffled together and attended these classes jointly. Manjot attended all her classes regularly except her Hindi class. "I didn't even know who my Hindi teacher was", she said.

Ragging was quite an intrinsic part of first-year life in both college and the hostel. Initially, she disliked being ragged, but later realised that it wasn't that bad, and it helped her learn the finer nuances of her art practice. "They asked us to do ten to twenty sketches in our sketchbooks every day, and they would check. They were like teachers in disguise". However, ragging also involved following the unpleasant instructions of the seniors, which irked Manjot and many of her friends. The juniors were asked to only dress up in suits, and this once led to a confrontation with her seniors that blew out of proportion. There were other forms of ragging, making the girls act like a newly wedded couple on their honeymoon, talk to lizards, and other unsavoury incidents. The ragging would often continue on college premises as well.

Despite these little hiccups, Manjot was thoroughly enjoying her college and hostel life. "I felt I had a world to explore, books to read and enjoy with friends. Hostel taught me how to be independent and how to organize myself and move on in life", she said. Second year onwards, the lessons were more focused towards painting, and Manjot, along with her friends, started spending more time on campus after classes were over. "At times, I would go into the library and read about artists and their works", said Manjot.

Manjot increasingly started focusing on developing her skills as an artist. Her still-life skills were quite strong from her school days, but she was very interested in compositions. "It took me a few years to get there", she said. She also took the help of her seniors, some of whom she'd already befriended, and asked them how to get the finer nuances right, like the color scheme, or proportions of the human body. By the fourth year, she said she became a master in making portraiture from life.

Manjot had a bunch of good friends in college. Shilpy (from Advertising) and Sonika (from Sculpture), both fellow hostel residents, were her closest friends. "We got in touch due to ragging. We would try to find ways to avoid ragging or find a solution to it", said Shilpy, whose room was next to Manjot's in the second year of college. "Both of us were from middle-class families and our traits matched. She was very positive. She had a spark to do something in life. In the second or third year, she told me about the book, *The Secret*, and said that whenever she gets stuck in life, she reads a page from it and finds a solution to her problem. She also made me watch the movie based on the book. I loved it".

A big break in Manjot's student-artist journey came in the third year of her college. A Sweden-based artist organization named Tellus-Art selected her for a two-week international artists' workshop in Stockholm. "A graduate from my own college was leading this workshop and wanted a student from our college to participate and I was chosen", she said. This trip marked several firsts for her: her maiden international journey, interaction with practising artists, and the opportunity to study

European art through its museums. She immersed herself in the works of Renaissance artists and contemporary European talents while exploring the art museums in Stockholm. "The visit had a great impact on my composition skills, my colour choices and how I worked after coming back from Sweden... There was a drastic change. I felt much more enriched", she said.

Her friend Shilpy also noticed the change in her friend's work. "There was a definite change in her work, and she never stopped after that". During her time in college, Manjot also watched a lot of art films—historical as well as contemporary—along with her friends and that, she said, brought in another kind of awareness in her life which played a big role later in her art choices.

During this time, Manjot also realised that it was important for her to become more focused about what she wanted to do in life. She topped her class in painting, something she'd never concerned herself with much during her school life.

Finding Love

While Manjot was open and fun-loving and doing well in her studies, she wasn't interested in dating anyone. All that changed when she met Sumeet Verma. Sumeet was an engineer and was living and working in Chandigarh. He was seven years older than her, and yet, he was someone she found herself feeling comfortable with. The two had met at a common family function for the first time, but it was only a casual interaction. Later, the two met again in Chandigarh and stayed in touch. One reason for Manjot to fall for her partner, she said, was her situation at home, and another was Sumeet's kindness and attitude towards life. "We were from the lower middle class".

About her situation at home, and how Sumeet figured into it, she said:

> Mom was amazing. She was caring and nurturing, albeit a little strict. I had a great relationship with her. Dad was there as a constant support. He provided financial support, but he unknowingly suffered from alcoholism. I witnessed conflict at home between my mom and him. This put a lot

of psychological pressure on me, and I wanted to get out of the house. I wanted to be at a place which was peaceful and full of love.

When Sumeet came into her life, Manjot felt stable and loved. She was nineteen when he proposed to her first, but she turned him down. It was when she was taking care of her mom after her sudden hospitalization that she felt "severely alone and overwhelmed" by her circumstances and started chatting with Sumeet. I started getting the love and support I needed from him", she said.

Manjot soon told her parents about him, but they were extremely unhappy about their daughter's decision. Her mother said she thought her daughter was too young and wanted her to focus on her studies. "I was unhappy. They were just kids. She (Manjot) didn't know...", she reported. After graduation, Manjot wanted to go to Shantiniketan to pursue higher studies, but she dropped the idea after her mom's displeasure.

Her parents, however, looking at the couple's determination, decided to meet Sumeet's parents and formalize the relationship. "We went to Patiala and did her *roka,* but I told her in-laws that I won't let my daughter get married till she completes her graduation", said Ant*ji.* "Her in-laws are supportive. They didn't object at all. In fact, after she won the University gold medal in Master's in Fine Arts, they threw a huge party to celebrate her win".

FULL BLOOM

(Present)

Manjot enrolled for her master's program in the same college in 2011. "Initially during my master's, I didn't tell anyone that I was married. I wanted to change the perception of society, that girls cannot study or work after they get married", she said. Manjot also realised that marriage brought with it a lot of "boundaries and responsibilities". "My marriage was both a boon and a bane. I liked it initially, but I also felt overwhelmed". However, the newlyweds shared all household responsibilities. "There were hiccups, but we used to talk it out and resolve our differences", said Sumeet. "Manjot was serious about her work and extremely hard working. She had a bicycle, and during her exhibitions, she would ride her bike all across the town to arrange the materials she needed for the show. She also used to take extensive notes in diaries to help her improve her work".

Manjot was clear about wanting to pursue her master's and be financially independent. As an artist, she also dreamed of developing new ideas, travelling, and meeting other practising artists through residencies, and collaborating on national and international art projects. In the first year of her master's, Manjot was not only awarded a scholarship from Lalit Kala Academy, Chandigarh, but she also got a great opportunity to participate in an art workshop organised by them under the mentorship of Atul Dodiya, a famous contemporary visual artist living in Mumbai. Manjot was one of the twelve artists shortlisted for this prestigious workshop. "I got to understand how an artist proceeds in life. What happens after you finish college and how life moves on...Atul Dodiya is a humble artist and talked about these experiences in depth. This workshop was organized by Mr. Diwan Manna, a visual artist and Chairman of Chandigarh Lalit Kala Akademi. He also introduced me and my work to (Late) Professor B.N. Goswamy".

Later, (Late) Professor B.N. Goswamy, a world-renowned art historian and scholar who lives in Chandigarh, acquired her works. His lectures and books on Indian Miniature Painting also had a profound impact on her thinking. Manjot would often go to the Government Museum, Chandigarh, to look at the collection of Indian Miniatures. She was still struggling with the content of her paintings. "Why am I making paintings? What is it that I want to say to my audience? These were the questions I was struggling with", she said.

In the second year of her master's, Manjot won an award for her 2D animation art video. Earlier, she'd completed a short course during the three-month gap just after she completed her studies in senior-secondary school. This knowledge helped her create the 2D animation during her master's. She said:

> I was reading Sigmund Freud and Carl Jung. I was interested in learning how the human mind works, the

> conscious, subconscious and unconscious realms. I decided to engage in conversations with people while scribbling and drawing aimlessly. I didn't focus on creating meanings, simply letting my hand follow whatever forms emerged during these interactions. I did approximately forty or fifty works and called them "Untalkable Drawings", given that I was unsure what I was making. I displayed it in my class and asked my Professor Sanjeev Soni for his feedback. He didn't say much, rather suggested "what if these drawings could move", as he knew I had learnt animation. I found his suggestion intriguing. I digitised the work and started animating them. I was doing it randomly, moving any elements I felt like. After that was done, I thought the videos needed sound as well. I downloaded a bunch of random sounds from free sources on the internet and used them in the video, and then called them the "Untalkable Videos". I still didn't want to give meaning to these works". Whatever the audience wants to think about it, laugh about it, make fun of me...this is my expression.

Her work was selected for a prestigious award at Chandigarh Lalit Kala's annual art exhibition, under the student category. She also received compliments from the judge, Sudarshan Shetty, one of the leading visual artists of India who confided in Diwan Manna, then Chairman of Lalit Kala Academy, that if her work would have won an award even if it was presented in the professional category.

A Period of Doubt

After completing her master's in 2012, Manjot applied for a job at Chandigarh University. She started teaching 2D animation as an assistant professor to B.A. students. She worked there only for six months as she didn't receive job satisfaction and applied for a teaching job at Navodaya Vidyalaya. She got through both her written and interview examination. Manjot spent the next two years at Moga. "I was working because I wanted to become financially independent so that I could make my own decisions, and furthermore, I wanted to have the experience of studying from a reputed university abroad. I would usually think, what is that ability that makes people who have studied from Ivy League Universities unique, and desired to have those abilities for myself".

Along with her job, she started filling out applications to prestigious art universities for her PhD outside the country. "I was still not clear about the *why* of the content in my artworks. However, one thing that was clear to me was that the beauty of nature could not surpass my eye", she said.

In the meanwhile, her applications were being rejected. This was a tough period for her. She was living away from her husband in a small village where she hardly had any exposure to art galleries or other art events. "I had the desire to move back to my home in Chandigarh, live a city life, meet my friends, as well as be able to visit some art events", she said. During this time, the Chairperson of Lalit Kala Academy, Diwan Manna, was shaping the art scene of Chandigarh by bringing many renowned Indian and International artists to the city and organizing artist talks, conducting workshops and seminars, and sharing their work. Manjot heard about all this and said she had the "urge to be present at these gatherings".

She applied for another government job in Chandigarh, and again got through and shifted back to her city after two years in 2015. She also applied for a short-term project, a travelling artists' residency, where they travelled through rural Gujarat. This trip gave her a lot of insight into land and nature, and how nature impacts the art process. She was sure by then that nature would be the central aspect of her art. However, her artistic struggle continued even after that. "Things didn't come easy to me. I had to struggle. I kept telling myself, you have to keep going".

In 2014, Dr. (Late) B.N. Goswamy recommended her for a national artists' camp held at Dhirubhai Ambani Knowledge Centre, Mumbai. "They had invited 20 artists from all over India. We were to be there for three weeks and had to create two artworks", she said. It was an important landmark in her journey and gave her more confidence as an artist. "During the time I was applying for art residencies and art awards, I faced a lot of rejection, but some opportunities also knocked on my door", she said. I went to Kolkata in 2017 at the Kolkata International Performance Art Festival (KIPAF). Later, I also got another opportunity to travel to Switzerland for a Land-Art Residency".

Manjot had saved enough money from her teaching assignments to take care of her flight ticket and other travel expenses, while her residency took care of her food and stay. The title of the residency was "Mythos". It was in the centre of a forest and Manjot loved going for nature walks in the evenings, a habit that continues till today. "I traveled a lot in Switzerland. It was a lot of experimental work. I also explored different museums, especially in Basel, Bern, and Neuchatel, and explored the streets of these cities with awe and wonder. Switzerland looked like a fairytale land to me, something I had never seen before, and the picturesque landscapes still remain close to my heart", she said.

Exploring Art and the World

After her trip to Switzerland, what struck her the most upon her return was the pollution, congestion, and attitude of people. "I started thinking about the correlation between the attitudes of people living in developing and developed nations", she said. "These thoughts impact many aspects of my work today". From 2017–2019, she also worked part-time with Lalit Kala Academy, Chandigarh. It was during this time that she started working under Diwan Manna, a pioneer among art photographers in India and (the then) President of Lalit Kala Academy, Punjab. "I learned of her when she started participating in Lalit Kala Academy activities sometime in 2011", said Diwan Manna. "Her works were different. Her handling of material wasn't routine...One could make out she was different and committed. She would keep poking me about other aspects of art. It impressed me." Manjot adds, "For me, working with him was one of my life's best learning times. By working on various assignments related to documenting the events, organising workshops, interviewing Punjabi artists and editing catalogs,

I understood the finer nuances of intricacy, attention to detail, as well as an improvement in my vocabulary. It was under his indirect mentorship I learned more about the professional art world".

2018 proved to be lucky for her. For the past two years, she'd been applying for residency at the prestigious Khoj International Artists' Association, New Delhi. In 2018, she was one of the five artists selected for the residency, out of a total of 350 applications from across the country. "It was a national breakthrough for me. I got this recognition after five years of passing out of college. People started knowing about my work". It was an immersive experience for her, where she used 2D animation, installations, and scientific equipment like silver nitrate and copper wire to create an immersive art installation. "I was thinking about the fragility of human life, the idea of borderlines, and who creates them. I was also thinking about my motherhood choices and the extraction of resources. All this came together in an abstract way in my artwork through installations and 2D animation", she said.

While she was at Khoj, she got a beautiful email titled "Very very good news". Earlier that year, she had applied for a residency at Unidee, Fondazione Pistoletto, Biella in Italy, supported by Inlaks Shivdasani Foundation, India. She was a stand-alone fellow for this fully-funded residency, representing India. Later, in 2018, in the months of September, October and November, Manjot spent her time in Italy, where she had the brilliant opportunity to meet three other women artists from Azerbaijan, Palestine and Ecuador. "We had in-depth conversations about our cultural differences and similarities, as well as what it means to be women and carving paths as women artists." She also visited leading art institutions and museums in Turin, Venice, Milan, Florence, Rome, and Palermo.

Finding her Niche

"It had been 8 years of my marriage, and I started to find myself surrounded with questions related to childbirth and motherhood. I was still not certain if I wanted to have children. I wanted to explore other possible ways of living". It did cause some friction with her husband and extended family members, however she wanted to listen to her heart and mind. She said:

> I knew bearing a child comes with a lot of responsibility, and I was not sure if I wanted to take this responsibility yet. Given these questions, I started looking at larger issues like how humans impact the environment, how India is on the brink of becoming the world's most populated country, and how people are struggling for resources. It also intrigued me to bring these issues in my art practice. I was thinking about questions like the consequences of fertility, and the urge to procreate for the human species.

Another fantastic opportunity came to her just before the pandemic struck. She was chosen as an artist-in-residence at the extremely prestigious Jan van Eyck Academie, Maastricht, Netherlands (2020-21). However, her arrival at Jan van Eyck Academie was one big adventure which involved a long wait and renewing her visa for the Netherlands (as the first one had expired due to the Covid pandemic). During the pandemic, Manjot lived by herself in her house in Chandigarh, as Sumeet had already shifted to Vancouver by then and her parents and in-laws were living in different cities. She turned the rest of the house into her studio. She had all the materials she needed. "I asked myself, what is Nature trying to tell human beings? Is the pandemic because of the numbers and enormous growth that has happened in the last 100 years? It brought in another kind of awakening that wildlife needs space", she said. About her artistic motivations, she added:

> It was like the dots started to connect. My preoccupation with ecology, finding alternative meanings for motherhood, and resource extraction started to make more sense. To beat my loneliness during Covid-19, I turned once again to painting. It was now that the issues related to motherhood, fertility of humans, as well as nature started surfacing in my painting. I painted the image of goddess Lajja Gauri, where I depicted her giving birth to an ecosystem, and not a human child. For me, this was a landmark moment as it brought clarity of thought to how I want to proceed further as an artist.

She started depicting all her reflections through miniature paintings on the interdependence of multispecies, which is a predominant and recurring theme in her paintings now. It was the pandemic that forced her to specifically focus on painting. Her year-long stint at the Jan van Eyck Academie, Netherlands—where she found all the support an artist needed in one place, including a dedicated studio space, an international community of emerging and established artists, mentorship from world renowned artists, writers, and curators—reinforced her conviction about her preoccupation with nature and the way forward in her artistic journey. Manjot now lives between Vancouver, Canada and Chandigarh, India. She said her paintings aim to open possibilities for a post-queer and post-human world, where beings move towards an uncanny kind of becoming in a multispecies world.

She is constantly becoming sharper and more nuanced with time, and now she has full faith in her work. "My thinking about Nature, Environmental Justice, and Ecology informs my art practice. I know this is my way forward", she said.

Diwan Manna sums up Manjot's journey as an artist, "She's constantly growing. She is dedicated, more focused, and articulate and constantly writes about her work. Her art practice is growing."

6
Nida Mahmood

Fashion Designer, Graphic Designer & Interior Designer

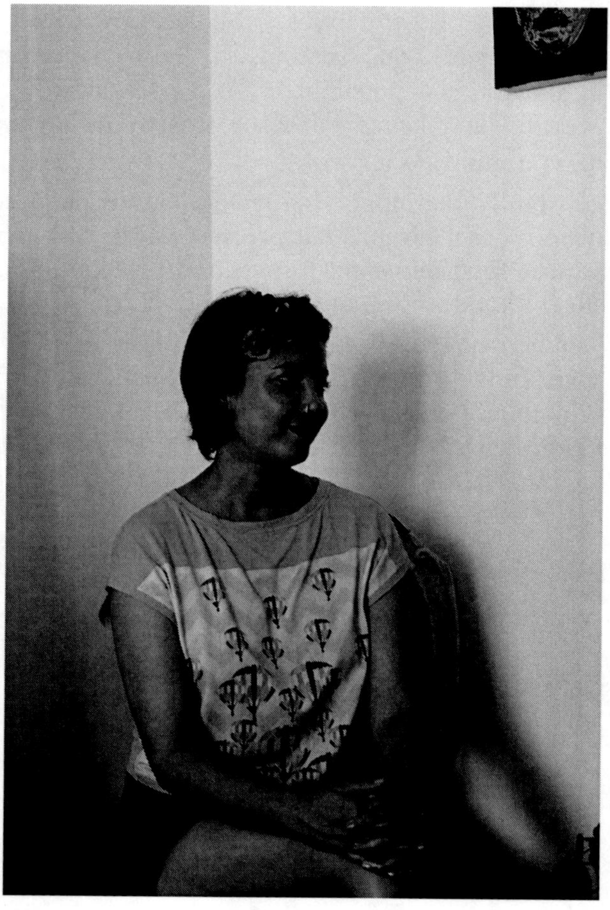

Figure 6

"I'm inspired by simple things. Indian things. Grassroots India is what I like...I've brought Kitsch into mainstream."

—Nida Mahmood

NIDA MAHMOOD (b. 1982), hailed as the "Queen of Kitsch" by the Indian media, is a designer who dabbles in Fashion, Graphics, Art, Film, Installation, Interiors, et al. As a trained designer from NIFT, whose collection was awarded the "Most Creative Design Collection" in 2002, her innovative thinking and creative prowess have acceded her with several prestigious and successful collaborations in a short span of time and brought her international recognition.

Some of the famous brands she's designed for or collaborated with over the years are Lady Gaga, Godrej Design Lab, Victoria and Albert Museum, Taj Vivanta, Absolut for art installations, Nike for a special range of apparel for the cricket world cup, and more. Many other brands like Blenders Pride, Swarovski, NDTV Good Times, HCL, and Adidas are also her prominent clients. She has also conceptualized and designed the restaurant Junglee Billee (in Delhi) and created art installations for Harley Davidson and Channel V. She designed a line of high-end limited edition designer jackets for the Superbike World Championship. Her collaboration with Satya Paul and sports lux line for Deivee in collaboration with Milind Soman received rave reviews and were a commercial success. Her collaboration with the jewellery line Swarovski's Confluence with India-inspired designs received critical acclaim and was a great success. She created a very interesting graphic collaboration with Johnnie Walker for the prestigious John Legend and Raja Kumari India tour.

A multi-talented artist, Nida describes her childhood self as someone who was sincere, creative and often liked to "drift into her make-belief world". While she always knew that she wanted to do something creative with her life, it was not until her senior secondary years, when a classmate mentioned NIFT, that she got interested in Fashion Design and was convinced that it was the right path for her. Through her incredible story, readers will gain an insight into how a student of science, excelling in academics, almost set to take the medical entrance exam and study medicine, suddenly turned to fashion design, finding her unique offering to the world of design and became a name to reckon with.

STAR BUD

(Childhood)

Nida was born and brought up in Lucknow in a family where, she said, girls are given more importance than boys. Her late father, Mr. N.H. Faruqi, was a geologist (who later retired as the Director General of the Geological Survey of India), and her mother, Mrs. Safia Faruqi, a teacher (now retired), were both nature lovers, and so it was natural for Nida to be attracted to plants and animals from a young age. She said her love for animals comes from her dad, who loved dogs.

One of her first memories of childhood is of her 1st birthday; her cake had a rooster and a hen on it (because she used to love them as a child). Later, for one of her design collections, her muse was a rooster, and the idea behind the collection was a surreal take on dreamscapes. The collection was an ode to her psychedelic and vivid dreams.

Nida feels that she has imbibed a lot of qualities from her father, like being organized, punctual, focused, dependable, and straightforward. However, it is her mother who has had the biggest influence on her during her childhood and adolescence, and she shares a close bond with her even now. "I remember distinctly how enamoured I was with my mother. She was so pretty!", she said. A voracious reader, Nida disclosed that her love for English literature and poetry "evolved and flourished" from childhood because of her mother, which later graduated to philosophy, metaphysics and spirituality.

From the beginning, Nida was a self-assured girl who believed she could achieve anything. Her parents also encouraged her to take up activities she found interesting outside of her studies. She was a brilliant student, an excellent debater, and equally good at sports. "I must have dabbled in everything from art to sports, drama and singing. I was a very outgoing and confident girl. I think I was brought up to be my own person without any hang-ups and was taught to explore everything that I found interesting. I was always a very diligent, persevering child", she said.

Nida's mother, Safia*ji,* described her daughter as a girl who took centre stage and entertained their guests with interesting conversations. "I never had to scold her. She was very organized always and still is...her projects were elaborately made. We were very proud of her for being good at studies, games and extracurriculars. She loved drawing, and her work was displayed at many prominent spots in school. I was known as Nida's mother when I joined her school as an ISC English teacher", she said. "Moreover, her little brother (Usman, seven years younger than Nida) adored her", Safia*ji* added. "She would take it upon herself to get his uniform ready when he started going to school. Both have been thick as thieves".

About her relationship with her younger brother, Nida says that they were very close. However, it was a typical "who-can-bully-who" relationship when they were kids. "I bullied him when he was little, but once he was a bit grown up, he totally emotionally bullied me into doing things for him. He totally took advantage of my love for him as a kid and continues to do so even today", she said. Usman, on his part, accepted that his sister has been more like a mother to him besides also being his closest ally. "She always backed me up and got me permission from dad for special events or school outings". The siblings also studied in the same school. Usman said that whenever he was bullied by his seniors, he would complain to his sister (who was the President of the Students Welfare Committee), and she would ensure that no one troubled her brother.

Discovering Design

Nida excelled in studies and dabbled in almost everything that interested her during her school life. Nida's English teacher, Ms. Sandra Godin, had this to say about her ex-student:

> Nida was a child who stood out from the rest of the girls because of her mannerisms. She was very deliberate in her speech and actions and did not speak randomly. She was a rather poised girl, and never raucous or brash! I remember watching her and being surprised at the aura of dreamy thoughtfulness she exuded. She was thorough in everything she did. She was also kind-hearted, as I remember her volunteering to help a fellow classmate finish her history project by sacrificing her break and library period. I have nothing but admiration for Nida.

Despite doing well in academics, Nida said she knew she would do something creative with her life. "I didn't know how to define it while in school, but subconsciously, I was sure I would find my path. With so much interest in so many diverse activities, it was not hard to know that life would be interesting along the way", she said.

In fact, as a science student for a long time, almost everyone around her (including herself) believed she would end up as a doctor like many of her cousins. In her senior secondary years, she'd also started preparing for her medical entrance test. It was around this time that a fellow student mentioned going to NIFT to her.

In a city like Lucknow, Fashion Design as a career option was unheard of, but Nida was intrigued and found herself increasingly drawn to the idea of completing a course in fashion design from the prestigious NIFT, Hyderabad.

She said it was a life-altering experience for her as she couldn't see herself spending the rest of her life as a doctor. She spoke about her interest and desire to pursue a course in fashion design with her parents, who were again encouraging and asked her to take the exam.

In fact, her father told her that if she worked hard and cleared the NIFT entrance, there was nothing that could come in her way. She said, "I have never shied away from toiling hard and making sure I achieve the goal I have set out to achieve. This, I feel, is the most powerful takeaway from my childhood". This attitude helped her throughout her periods of struggle and beyond, and became one of the primary reasons—apart from her inherent talent—for her stupendous success as a young fashion designer in the country.

RAY FLORET

(Youth)

Nida clearing the written entrance test for NIFT was a big win and a happy occasion for her and her family. However, she recalled that it wasn't all that simple. She had no idea what was to be done after the written test. The situational test and interview were to be conducted in Delhi. Her mother tried to seek information from others, but it wasn't much help. Yet, along with her mother's help, she prepared her first portfolio with some quality work. She had no formal art training, but she said that the portfolio came out nice, as she included some of her works on still life—something she was particularly good at.

"Looking back, I realize that I didn't have a single nervous or scared bone in my body. It felt like a breeze at that point, in retrospect. I'm amazed how confidence can completely change the game!", she said. Nida's situational test went well. It was followed by a forty-five-minute-long interview with the jury the next day.

She said that some of the professors who were part of her jury later became valuable mentors while at NIFT and afterwards when she moved to Delhi and started her journey as an independent designer.

Hard Work Paying Off

"NIFT was fun. The whole world seemed to have changed for me overnight. Pursuing a creative dream was so overpowering that I was grateful every single day for having found my way to design school", she said. She spent most of her three years in NIFT working diligently. "No *chai* breaks or smoke breaks for me. I don't smoke, so it seemed like a pointless waste of time. I was so engaged in my work most of the time, that I genuinely didn't care to take breaks. The lunch break was an odd fit shoved somewhere because it had to be incorporated", she disclosed. In fact, Nida said that she was enjoying herself so much upon finding her calling and initiating her creative journey that she couldn't have enough of it. She also credits NIFT for the mental and creative transformation she underwent during her time there.

Professor Sanjay Shrivastava, who taught Nida's batch and is currently the Director of NIFT, Patna, said it was clear to him from the beginning that Nida was destined for significant accomplishments in her domain area and beyond.

"As an educator, I have watched her grow and observed her talents and interests. She has an excellent balance of analytical and creative thinking skills and a great eye for detail. She was an exceptional student and a great learner", he said. He went on to add that Nida was a diligent student and quickly learned to manage her time, managed to work in group situations under strict deadlines, and recognized the importance of a strong work ethic, persistence, leadership, and intellectual integrity. During her study assignments outside the four walls of NIFT, she always gave new design ideas for better business opportunities.

At NIFT, Nida's dedication and innate ability to come up with unique design ideas paid off and she won the Most Creative Design Collection Award in 2002. "Her design collection was intense," said her friend, Angie Dhillon, who met Nida in NIFT. The two became good friends from the first moment, as they both had the same bent of mind. "I remember she'd made a very elaborate collection with 30 odd pieces while the requirement was to make 5-7 ensembles. The collection was detailed with multiple surface structures and self-development prints, complex pattern making and a very interesting concept. It was inspired by Schizophrenia. I think it was a very interesting collection".

FULL BLOOM

(Present)

After finishing her course at NIFT in 2002, Nida shifted to Mumbai. She said she chose to work in Mumbai to gain new exposure and experience. Hungry to learn fast, Nida chose to work with two different companies in morning and evening shifts. However, what worked in her favour was her living arrangement. She said she was lucky to find the perfect hostel for herself. While on her way to Mumbai, she met someone on the train who guided her to the Villa Theresa Girls Hostel on Pedder Road, South Mumbai. Not only did they have a vacancy, but Nida managed to get an independent room for herself. Her evening workplace was across the road from her hostel. In a metro city like Mumbai, this was a huge advantage.

A large part of Nida's life in Mumbai revolved around her work, and she had little time for leisure activities, which she didn't mind. Consequently, her friend circle was also limited. However, Nida did find a good friend in Pallavi Hasariya, who had also just started her first job and had moved to the same hostel a couple of weeks before her. Soon, the two became good friends and spent their spare time together. Even after all these years, the two have maintained their friendship.

Pallavi Hasariya shared how the two friends first met each other:

> We met in the common area of the hostel, struck up a conversation, and immediately liked each other, even though we were from different worlds. Coming from a traditional Rajasthani family, I knew that in all likelihood, I would also get married and stay home like my sisters after working for a few years. It was all temporary. Nida, on the other hand, was all into her work, career and future. She was a NIFT topper. She was so passionate about the fashion world, and she wanted to make a difference! I would tell her all about realistic stories from my world, and she would share all these futuristic stories from her world and how she wants to make it big. I understood her creative world well, and both of us loved dressing up! I also remember shopping together and buying the same tops that we would wear on the same day! I remember her being very disciplined, whether it came to healthy eating or saying her prayers or keeping the schedule. Most folks at this hostel loved her!

Pallavi went on to add that while Nida became her fashion coach, she familiarized her friend with Mumbai.

Progressing towards her Dreams

In 2003, Nida married a Delhi-based lawyer, Saif Mahmood, and shifted to the capital city. After working for others for a few years in Delhi, Nida started as an independent artist-designer. However, her initial years were filled with different kinds of challenges. She felt lost and clueless as a designer. She also didn't have money to participate in fashion week. "I didn't know what my designs should be like and what they should represent", she said.

"It took me a full year to figure out what my design sensibility truly was, and within this span of time I got a fantastic art project that gave me enough seed money to get into mainstream fashion. My first show, "High on Chai", happened and it jumpstarted me into the glitzy world of fashion. Many wonderful people in the shape of buyers, press (who wrote amazing things about my work), and friends who helped me grow as a designer came along as the juggernaut propelled me in the right direction", she said. Nida shared how a simple observation seeded the idea for her first unique collection, "High on Chai".

In 2009, FDCI informed Nida that she was selected for the Wills Lifestyle India Fashion Week to present her first collection. Nida was happy to be selected but had no clue what she would present for her first show. One day, after parking her car in a street close to her office, she casually glanced at a chai stall with a bright yellow tarpaulin roof. People were sitting around the stall on an old bench and drinking tea. She said she just stood there oblivious to everything else, absorbing the colourful scene in front of her, when suddenly it struck her that she wanted to paint this exact picture through her collection and bring the chai culture of India alive. It was a 'Eureka moment' for her.

She worked on the quirky idea for her first show along with three tailors with the limited budget and time she had. Her creative collection "High on Chai" was not only a massive success with the buyers but also with the media. "My favourite was this story from HT City. The caption read, "Creativity outburst, finally". It talked about my show in a beautiful way. It is safe to say that my show had overshadowed the finale in the media reports that season", she said. It was only after the success of her first collection that Nida understood herself as an artist and designer and started her journey for the quest for all things India.

Since then, Nida has worked on several prestigious creative projects, in many of which she has presented grassroots India and its myriad shades, showcasing true India through her art. Bollywood actor and model, Milind Soman, with whom she's worked closely on a unique project spread over a year, said:

> During the course of the project, we had the opportunity to work closely together on the line. It was a great experience in terms of professionalism as well as interaction with her as a person. I find her work fun and exciting. Her use of colours, and her knack with prints are unique. The whole experience was warm and hence, we have stayed in touch over the years.

Jamal Sheikh, Editor of HT Brunch, who, like Milind, met Nida through work and is also a good friend, vouches for Nida's work and says they're not only "socially relevant" and handled with a lot of "sensitivity", but are also "edgy and fun". "I think she is committed to a distinct style of work which creates its own statement", Jamal said.

Over the years, Nida has spent a lot of time honing her skills as an artist and a fashion designer. As an artist, she has dabbled in art, fashion, writing, interiors, specialized gardening, designing public spaces like restaurants, and much more. She said keeping abreast with trends and applying herself in many parallel creative universes helped her grow tremendously as a creative soul and a professional.

"When you focus on your desires and work hard to achieve a goal, the universe conspires to make it possible", she said. "I have lived this my entire life when I was not evolved enough to be aware of this, and also when I found spiritual growth and learned about this phenomenon". She attributes her success to the countless "wonderful people" who came along in her journey to help her move ahead in her professional growth. She also recalled how her ex-husband supported her during her struggles. "Perhaps, without him, my early years would have been very different. On so many counts, I am grateful to have had him as part of my early years while I was building this beautiful legacy, which made the Indian media fondly call me "The Queen of Kitsch".

AJ Singh, a socialite from Delhi and a good friend, praised Nida for her unique sense of style. "Despite her passion and dedication for her work as a designer, Nida is good at many things and is fun to be with", he added.

Challenging Intangibilities

When at home, Nida likes to spend time with nature. "I'm an avid gardener. It is very therapeutic to nurture and tend to my plants at home, and I have literally hundreds of plants. Sundays are usually spent gardening with my little partner, Mr. Toffee Tinkerbell, (her cat) in tow. A lot of simple things invigorate me as a creative person and then I'm ready to take on more." Nida also openly voices her opinion on women's rights, and supports the LGBTIQA+ community and talks about other issues she feels strongly about.

She continues to work on some unique ideas and concepts that are unheard of, and brings them to life. She said:

> I have worked on ideas that are absolutely intangible, but I have managed to translate them into collections, which have been well received and accepted not just by the media, but also commercially. This makes me realize that creative people have the ability to "create". The word "create" is not a small word. An intangible idea transforming into a tangible design and being sold is a brilliant space to be in. It is a beautiful creative high.

As her ex-husband Saif Mahmood puts it succinctly, "Nida has the gift of creating art from the mundane. She doesn't need a studio setting, paper to sketch on, or fabric to design. Perfectionist to a fault, she fashions her own beauty from the ordinary things of our humdrum existence. She is a fearlessly wandering soul—in life and art alike—unafraid of dreaming and daring to defy".

7

Pelva Naik

Dhrupad Vocalist

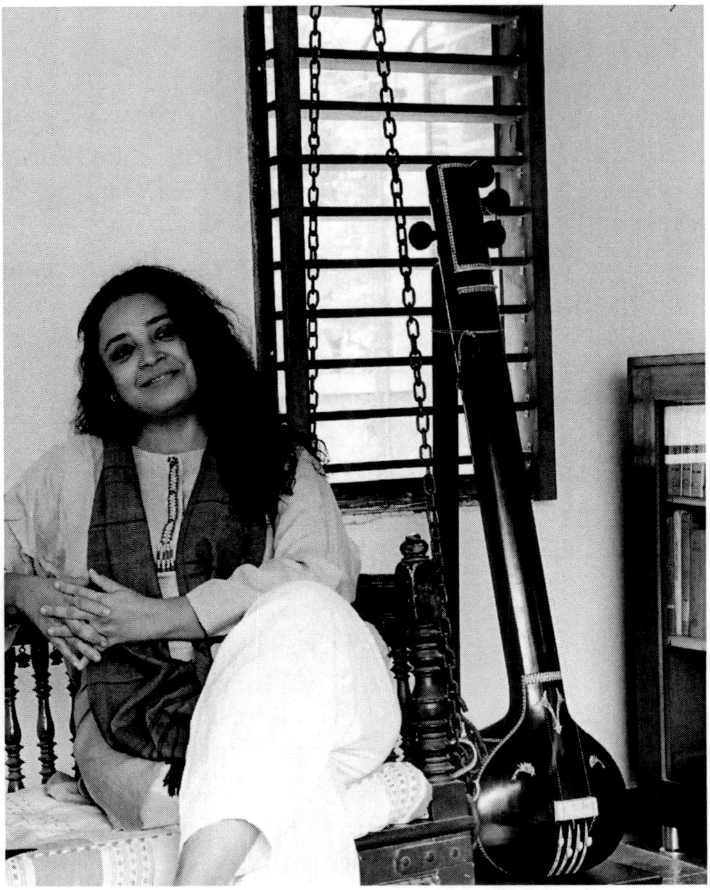

Figure 7

"I like to look at Dhrupad as a person or an organism. If you look at it like that, there's so much more to it than is visible. There's no limit to it."

—Pelva Naik

PELVA NAIK (b. 1986) is one of the leading young Indian Classical vocalists and an exponent of the ancient genre of classical Raga Music Tradition named Dhrupad. With an outstanding and ongoing stage career nationally and internationally, her work is inspired by her passion for re-discovering ancient sounds and her deep interest in historically informed performance practice and teaching.

Pelva's focus is to get to the heart of her music with a combination of depth, brilliance, and freedom. She is a student of life and art. Pelva hails from a family of artists and educators and has been trained in the Dhrupad style of vocal music under the eminent Dagar School of Indian Classical Music.

She began her training in Dhrupad at the age of seventeen. She is a disciple of legendary Dhrupad maestro Ustad Zia Fariduddin Dagar. She has also received able guidance from the Rudraveena exponent, Bahauddin Dagar. Pelva grew up singing and studying a wide spectrum of Indian folk songs, Gujarati literature, dance and fine arts. She began her formal training in Hindustani Khayal singing in Ahmedabad, under the tutelage of Senior Vocalist Smt. Pratima Trivedi. She went on to study fine arts and humanities at the Krishnamurti Foundation School in Bangalore, where she met Ustad Z.F. Dagar. Pelva is active in the fight against hierarchy in gender, class, caste, race, and religion in the field of arts, and society at large. The singer completed her master's degree in philosophy with distinction, and is also deeply interested in history, metaphysics, travelling, reading, writing, painting, and cooking.

In her music, Pelva endeavours to adhere sincerely to the unique traditional elements that the Dhrupad form offers. At the same time, she is known to strive to cultivate fresh characteristics that are personal and distinct. *Alāp*, the slow and intricate elaboration of a *Rāga,* is the hallmark of the Dagar school of Dhrupad Music. She takes particular interest in the exploration and formation of *Raga* in its most personal and uncharted features. Pelva believes teaching music, sharing, and upholding the sense of responsibility that comes with it is what keeps the process of evolution constant in craft and in life. Pelva is one of the most acclaimed and admired young Dhrupad teachers today due to her eloquent, easy manner, and her natural ability and passion to relate to every individual seeking to learn and listen to *Raga* music across the globe.

She has performed at several prominent and prestigious platforms: Theatre De La Ville in Paris (2017), Festival De Fes in Morocco (2017), Darbar Festival at South Bank Centre in London (2015), Summer Mela for Alan Danielle Foundation in Rome and Venice (2017), Ravenna Festival in Italy (2017), Prithvi Theater in Mumbai (2016 and 2022), First Edition Arts in Mumbai (2016), The 71st Doverlane Music Conference in Kolkata (2023), World Sacred Spirit Festival in Jodhpur (2019), Kiran Nadar Museum of Art in New Delhi (2022), G5A Warehouse in Mumbai (2022), Labyrinth Catalunya in Spain (2023 and 2024).

STARBUD

(Childhood)

Pelva was born in Ahmedabad in a family where literature, music and art were encouraged and celebrated as a way of life even before she was born. While her father, Paresh Naik, is a freelance writer and filmmaker, her mother, Vibha Naik, was a teacher and retired in 2021 as the principal of a school where she taught language. Vibha*ji* had a keen interest in literature and the performing arts (being a dancer herself), and she and her husband inculcated the same values in their daughter. "As a child, Pelva was very enthusiastic, cheerful, calm, and confident. Singing was her passion from a very early age. She would listen to a lot of music that was regularly played in our house. We, too, sang by habit", said Vibha*ji*, describing her daughter's nature and love for music.

Pelva was greatly influenced by her maternal grandmother during her childhood. Her grandmother had a school of her own, where an alternative form of education was disseminated, including teaching vernacular languages to students. Pelva was admitted to Sharda Mandir, one of the oldest schools in Gujarat, well known for its focus on music and vernacular languages. "My foundation was vernacular. We were not business-centric", said Pelva. "They (my family) were all scholars and artists. There was a lot of folk singing too". It was no surprise that from a young age, Pelva was learning Kathak, Khayal and miniature painting. She started performing on stage at the age of fifteen. During the Navratri festival, she loved performing Garba at school. While she was inclined towards music and dance, she said she never wanted to become a musician or a dancer. The reason was that music and dance to her were "personal and so much more of an organic process". However, she said she definitely wanted to be a painter as she not only enjoyed painting but was also quite good at it.

Pelva described her relationship with her parents as being quite intimate. "There was an immense amount of freedom and a lot of communication with them", she said. "First an individual, then a gender, and then something else, that was my foundation". Pelva described herself as a quiet child who liked to spend a lot of time on her own. She had a few friendships, but mostly remained aloof and lost in her own world. She was good at studies, especially in the arts and languages, but math was her Achilles heel. Her father, Paresh*ji*, described his daughter as a very observant child who always had the patience to imbibe and absorb details. Vibha*ji* shared an incident from Pelva's childhood to show her daughter's presence of mind and quick-wittedness. "At the age of 11 or 12, once she and her best friend bicycled their way to play lawn tennis early in the morning. Half an hour later, we got a call on the landline. Pelva was on the line, and I was stunned to hear what she told me", said Vibha*ji*.

> What had happened was that soon after they started practising their game on the court, her friend fell and hurt herself badly, fracturing her leg in the process.

> Pelva first reached up to the phone booth, called her parents and called us using the money she had for the bicycle expenses. Her friend's parents were doctors and had already left for the clinic. She then supported her friend till the main road, waited till they could get an auto rickshaw, put her in the auto and took her to an orthopaedic surgeon. She could accomplish all these due to her quick insight into the situation, her confidence, her commitment and her *Dharmabuddhi*! Even I ended up learning a lesson.

Pelva was also a highly imaginative person as a child. "She had a motley of playthings which were spread out in front of her like an army, following her command as a teacher", said Paresh*ji*. "She was a master, or a teacher to her toys. Both human and animal images, laid out in front of her like an assembly of her very personal puppets. She would make eye contact with her dolls very sincerely, and I presume most of them looked back at her equally animatedly!" Pelva enjoyed being active, and liked being regularly assigned tasks and jobs, and being talked to like an equal. She'd be most happy to read aloud paragraphs or pages from the books she was reading to her parents. She'd constantly look forward to being given responsibilities, including those of others.

Leaving the Nest

In 2001, after completing her secondary education in Ahmedabad, Pelva took admission in Valley School, Bangalore, as the schools in Gujarat did not offer Humanities. "I went to a Gujarati-medium school and read Hindi books till I went to Bangalore for my senior secondary", she said.

Bangalore was a complete shift from the kind of environment she'd grown up in, but she was equally happy there and enjoyed the learning experience. She was good at art from childhood and was keen to pursue it, so she started contemplating taking up Fine Arts in college. "Valley School had a lovely campus...and I was preparing a portfolio for Fine Arts", she said. The school offered a special one-year post-school programme for students who were keen to explore diverse creative opportunities and learn new skills. Pelva decided to enroll for the post-school programme after her board exams.

It was during this period that she met her guru, Ustad Zia Fariddudin Dagar, an Indian classical vocalist belonging to the Dhrupad tradition of music. Ustad Zia Faridduin*ji* represented the 19th generation of the Dagar family of musicians, and was the torchbearer of the Gharana till his passing away a few years ago. After his death, his nephew Bahauddin has carried forward the mantle of the Gharana. Ustad had been invited by Valley School for their post-school programme to impart a workshop along with Bahauddin*ji*, who, at that time, was training under his uncle. The event was organized by Dr. Rupa Devadasan, who was Pelva's house parent during the year-long post-school programme and was the one to introduce her to Ustad Zia Fariddudin Dagar. "Since then, she (Dr. Devadasan) has seen me closely through my journey in art, music and life", said Pelva about her connection with Rupa*ji*, a doctor by profession who became an academician and taught science in Valley School.

A Change of Heart

Pelva was so moved by Ustad Faridduin's performance and the workshop he gave at her school that she gave up her earlier plans of pursuing Fine Arts and instead, she decided to attend a month-long workshop in Mumbai which Ustad was imparting to select students.

"I wanted to learn and be under the Ustad, my master", she said. Her parents, looking at her keenness, were fully supportive of her. Pelva attended the month-long rigorous workshop in Panvel, Mumbai, under Ustad Faridduin. She was one of the eight chosen students, comprising 4 girls and 4 boys, to attend the workshop. "It wasn't like a commercial workshop. Ustad was a traditional teacher. He basically adopted me", she said.

Pelva's determination to become a Dhrupad vocalist grew stronger after the workshop. When the workshop came to an end, Pelva's parents travelled to Panvel to bring back their daughter. Her father met Ustad Faridduin, and after the brief but "beautiful" interaction, he promised Ustad*ji* that his daughter would learn Dhrupad. "From early childhood, Pelva was exploring many disciplines of fine arts. But at some point, she laid down her preference for Dhrupad", said Vibha*ji*. "I can recall the time when she passed out from the Valley School in Bangalore and decided to go to IIT Powai to learn music. There was some churning in her young mind over the two different ideologies, but she was determined to find the light on this path".

RAY FLORET

(Youth)

In 2003, Ustad Fariuddin*ji* was invited as a guest professor at IIT Powai, Mumbai. At that time, the central government had a scheme under which legendary musicians would be hosted in places like IIT, IIM, and other reputed institutes. By this time, Pelva had also made up her mind to learn Dhrupad from Ustad*ji*. She followed him there and became his disciple. Vibha*ji* recalls the role they had to play as parents to support their daughter's unique journey:

> "After she completed the three years of the post-school programme at the Valley School, Pelva and her father travelled across India to assess the potential and possibilities of pursuing fine arts. Soon after that, she attended the workshop on Dhrupad at the Valley School, conducted by Ustad Zia Fariduddin Dagar. Following this, she discussed with us on the phone her feelings of deep empathy and attachment towards learning Dhrupad. She also showed her preparedness for learning Dhrupad under the Gurukul tradition. We then further discussed with her teacher, Kabir Jayatirtha (of Valley School), the multiple dimensions involved in such a journey of learning.

New Roles and Routines

Pelva was one of Ustad's personal disciples and lived with him for two or three others on the Powai campus. She was the only girl, and there was no music fee specified. "Ustad was old school", she said. "He did not ask for any specific amount. It was all very casual".

Under her master, her routine life was vastly different than what she'd been used to, forcing Pelva to make necessary changes in her lifestyle. The routine she'd been following before she joined her masters was easier for her. She was used to being her own person, and doing her own thing in Bangalore and Ahmedabad. However, being the only female disciple, she had little privacy and no separate place to change or dress up. "I used to sleep in the music room", she said. However, she soon learnt to adjust to her new environment. "The only thing I knew was that I absolutely loved that form", she said. "When you're trying to learn something, you need to be totally naked. You develop a process of non-ego". She made friends with a couple of young men, who, like her, were also Ustad's personal disciples.

There was a great age divide between her guru, who was around seventy, and her, and yet she said there was intimacy when the musical exchange happened between them. At other times, she said she was like a small child trying to absorb everything. "It was a special and intimate relationship with my guru". Her master's tenure at IIT Powai was for two years, and she, along with a couple of other male students, stayed with their guru till the end of his tenure.

In 2006, Ustad Faridduin*ji* retired from IIT Powai, and shifted back to the Panvel Gurukul, which was also his elder brother's house. Pelva, too, shifted with him and a few other students. She said it was much homelier, and she felt an attachment to her Ustad's home. Work was delegated among the disciples. "Cooking and cleaning and music went hand-in-hand. What was taught in cooking was learnt in music", Pelva said. Pelva also started travelling to all the nooks and corners of the country with her guru. "Performances happened but were not the primary thing. Ustad used to push me to sing, and I would just jump in", she said. During this time, she came in proximity with Bahauddin, who was also under his uncle's tutelage, and was already an accomplished Rudraveena player. "I was a private person, but my teacher's nephew (Bahauddin) was someone I opened up to". She also found it enriching to imbibe the Veena qualities into her gayaki.

By this time, Pelva was in her early twenties, and her surroundings were shaping her up as an artist as well as a woman. She said she began to question herself and others: why do women have to sit cross-legged, and why are they raised differently than men? Earlier, she'd been used to dressing up as she liked, but in Panvel, she was only wearing simple Kurta-Pajamas with a dupatta. However, about her guru, she said, "My Ustad was also radical and felt women must be strong in communicating their opinions". Pelva disclosed that, for a long time, she was quite "submissive" and "giving" and "made adjustments" as she was still settling in her new ecosystem. "But when I realised the imbalance, I rebelled. I'm fearless in my approach and fiercely independent. I won't even ask my parents".

FULL BLOOM

(Present)

Pelva continued to stay with Ustad at Panvel, refining her Dhrupad Gayaki, but she'd also started teaching and performing solo from 2009–2010. Consequently, she was travelling a lot and spending less time in Panvel. She was teaching in Banaras and Bangalore, and giving small workshops at other places. In 2013, Ustad Zia Faridduin passed away. Pelva said he kept guiding her even until a few months before his death.

Widespread Recognition

Pelva's first big recognition as a Dhrupad vocalist came when she performed at the Darbar Festival in London in 2015. It was also her first trip abroad. After her success at the London Darbar Festival, Pelva was invited to many prestigious national and international festivals and musical events including Festival Gayatri, First Edition Arts, Mumbai (2016), Suburban Music Circle, Mumbai (2016), Theatre De La Ville, Paris (2017),

Darbar Festival in Ravenna, Italy (2017), Lalit Kala Academy Symposium Inaugural Concert, Kochi (2017), Festival Arambh by Raza Foundation, New Delhi (2018), Dhrupad Vaibhav, Raza Foundation, New Delhi (2019) to name a few. However, Pelva said that her actual earnings started only in 2015. Before that, while she'd started doing solo shows and was also teaching, it was her parents who were supporting her for the most part.

Paresh*ji* said about his daughter's musical journey:

> For Pelva, the entire journey was frequently filled with challenges, constantly hazardous, and many times, it was nearly impossible to proceed further. I guess, mostly, she didn't look at them as situations that were impossible to overcome, and worked her way around and out rather smoothly! Pelva often chooses to take up challenges willingly, that is, if she feels that's the only route leading up to her path. That doesn't mean she is 'ambitious' in the prevalent sense of the word. Rather, she experiments more than she calculates. This whole process has been very complex for her as well as for us, who witnessed or participated in it.

Preparing for Change

Pelva realised that a decade had gone by during which her horizon of knowledge about music and life had expanded, thanks to her Guru. Her views on art and music, artistic expression, practice and performance were exploding with richness. They say that a guru's death is not an ordinary one; it leaves behind potent forces of transformation if one holds the right insight to evolve out of it. Pelva experienced the same transformation within herself after the Ustad's death.

"I was ready. I thought I was. Nonetheless, there was much that I needed to introspect on. There was fear, there was a deep sense of attachment, and a strange sense of vanity that was forming which took another decade for me to emerge out of", she said. She recalls this time, disclosing:

> I took an unnecessary burden upon myself to look after the Gurukul. This was the time I was beginning to perform professionally. My communication and

> bond with my parents was being compromised and I was spreading myself too thin in terms of my physical, emotional and spiritual well-being. It took a long, turbulent few years for me to realise that I needed to come back to myself.

Brand New Beginnings

In 2019, she left the Gurukul. "It's been two years now of being constantly in the state of relentless introversion and self-examination. In this time, I have broken promises, moral convictions, hearts, friendships...but above all this, I have broken free", she said.

She has dedicated herself completely to art and music, which she feels are a medium to redefine and review the existential riddles she faces.

> Life is much greater than art, greater than legacies, cultures and even the idea of the divine. I am ready to create this music from a fresh, personal, and liberated perspective: The *Dagar Vāni Dhrupad*. This magnificent vehicle of *Raga* Music has some uncharted territories and elements to offer to humankind. I am looking forward to sing and share, love, nourish, sweat, strive, and remain constant on this path, directed by the light of the masters and by all the living and nonliving entities of Mother Earth, till my last breath.

She adds, "I was always into syllables. It was not only the act of singing but how you perceive the form. Singing gave me an immense sense of joy". Pelva's personal experiences have also impacted the way she sings and looks at art. The roots (of *Dhrupad Gayaki*) are there, and yet, she's able to find something new, and create from a completely fresh perspective. "Heritage is not something you preserve, it's something you keep alive even if it involves breaking the structure. I've been exploring sounds where I try to understand Dhrupad and understand my master. I'm able to create and innovate something of my own".

Subhayue, a Yoga Breath Trainer and Composer/Musician, and now a good friend of Pelva's, first met her during the first wave of Covid. The two have collaborated on different projects since then. He describes her beautifully: "The most important thing about Pelva is that she acts like a waterfall with art and life, always true to herself and flowing naked and wild. She's one of the true art practitioners in this age without the fear of a superficial orthodox structure".

8

Pragya Jain

Visual Artist & Entrepreneur

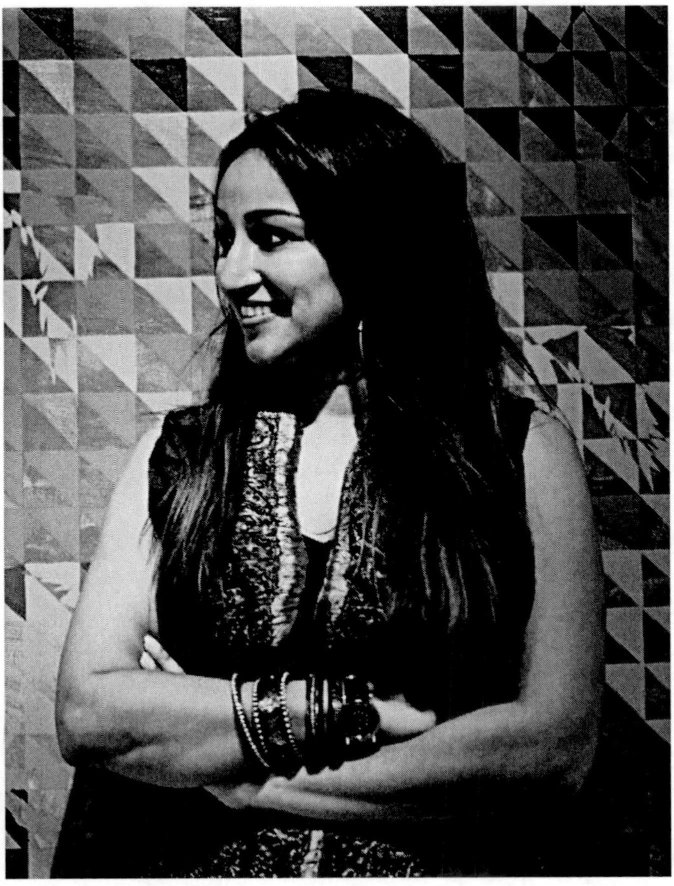

Figure 8

"To me, art is telling an uninterrupted story on the canvas."

—Pragya Jain

PRAGYA JAIN (b. 1984), a graduate of the Delhi College of Art, New Delhi, has been evolving as an artist in the Fine Arts field since 2001. Her works have been commended and appreciated since her days as a student. In high school, she was awarded by the President of India for excellence in Fine Art. Pragya's first solo exhibition in Bangalore, held in November 2009, brought her great appreciation and various art opportunities. Her works are a part of several collections and with notable art connoisseurs, such as the Jindals, the Prestige Group in India, and several art collectors globally.

A creative and thinking artist par excellence, Pragya made a flying start with her maiden art showing at a renowned art gallery in New Delhi that was proudly inaugurated by Nawab Pataudi. She, along with seven other women artists, created a 10×10 feet mural out of waste during the Covid-19 lockdown, and this now proudly is hanging on a prominent wall of the T3 terminal in New Delhi, as it caught the attention of the GVK group.

Her works were handpicked to be exhibited along with a number of Indian masters. At a later showing at Art Mall, New Delhi, Pragya made her acquaintance with art collectors, whose discerning eyes spotted the potential and promise her works held. Today, her works are in homes, offices of major collectors, and million-dollar apartment models all over India. Having shown her works at prestigious galleries in New York, Boston, and various other cities within the United States has given her artistic career immense stimulation.

In her mid-twenties, she volunteered at charitable organizations in multiple cities in North America that assist homeless people and provide them spaces to learn and create art. Pragya has been involved in teaching these struggling children and adults about the basics of art, and has helped them showcase their works. She is also the Vice President of the Pioneer Valley Chapter of the Women's Caucus for Art,

United States, which is a non-profit women's art organization with backing from the United Nations. She has actively curated and showcased in exhibitions that raise funds for the ill-fated in India, distributing Menstrual kits to over 500 young girls and ration kits to victimized families.

The growth pattern in her art is visible through a striving to explore. They reveal her findings through colours, design, and evocative imagery being integrated into a vision of grace, spirituality and happiness. It is the abstract works of Kandinsky and S.H. Raza inspired by inner beauty, the fervour of spirit, deep spiritual desire and inner necessity that inspire her subjects, colours and forms. Vibrant, bright colours and internal spiritual contexts make up Pragya's art. Looking out for fellow artists is another important aspect that drives her art. Pragya aspires to be known as a visionary optimistic artist in her life's path. In 2018, she co-founded an eco-conscious brand, Artychoke, with the intention of creating homeware and accessories adorned with her designs.

STARBUD

(Childhood)

Pragya Jain was born into an industrialist joint family in Delhi. She's the second of three siblings (she has an elder brother, Devashish and a younger sister, Anugya). Pragya's grandfather, Shri Bhiku Ram Jain, was a freedom fighter and a Member of Parliament from Chandni Chowk in 1983. Her father, Naren Bhiku Ram Jain, is an industrialist, a philanthropist, and the owner of an art gallery. Her mother, Ila Jain, is the co-founder of an eco-conscious homeware label, Artychoke, which she runs along with her daughters, Pragya & Anugya. Pragya said her childhood was spent in a house with "a massive family" and was all about everyday family dinners and endless fun activities with cousins. She recalled how she and her cousins had put up a show for their grandparents' 50th wedding anniversary for the grownups of the house. "The fifteen of us put up a show for the other twelve in the house. We made invites and prepared a skit and personalized songs for the whole family. We were always cooking up something", she said.

Pragya described her childhood as one with a relaxed and practical environment. "I grew up privileged. I had whatever I needed, but my parents never over-provided. We were kept far away from talks about money", she said. Pragya's brother, Devashish, said that their childhood was full of love and care. He described his sister as being shy but extremely gifted. "Pragya and I are very close in age and generally did a lot of things together. During our childhood, we spent a lot of time with our grandmothers in Delhi, as well as in Kolkata". Pragya's parents themselves are creative by nature and used to paint when they were younger. Pragya said both have been art enthusiasts and would collect paintings and sculptures for their home. Thus, art and music were encouraged from a very young age. "Both my parents have an eye for art, and I get it from them", she said. "My parents were quite clear about training me in all fields of art—music, drawing and dance".

Early Displays of Talent

Pragya was trained in Hindustani classical music and Kathak since she was four, and Western Music in her teenage years. "I used to sing classical and light songs for the All India Radio children and youth programmes that were aired", she said. Devashish revealed how his parents would put his sister on the spot at times, and ask her to sing a song in large gatherings, and she would have to charm the audience with her singing. "She's always been the sibling with so much talent, with singing and painting, but she was not always a big fan of showing it off".

In fact, as a child, Pragya wanted to pursue music as a career and even recorded songs for a TV programme in Mumbai. Naren*ji* shared that his daughter even auditioned for the singing reality show, *Indian Idol*, for season 1. However, as Pragya grew older, she realized that while she enjoyed singing, she didn't enjoy practising music for long hours, but what she really enjoyed was drawing and painting. She'd also started drawing at a very young age and was a "fast learner", said her father. She would happily sit for hours to draw. "I would be drawing and painting a lot during childhood. I could sit for six hours at a stretch to paint".

Pragya was admitted to Raghubir Singh Junior Modern School when she turned five, and moved to Modern School Barakhamba Road, New Delhi, in 6th grade. Her father, Naren*ji*, said that the principal was very impressed by Pragya at such a tender age. Her performance in academics was above average. She was a merit student in junior school, but her studies took a bit of a back seat during her senior school years. She said:

> A lot of things change in adolescence. I was this creative artsy child. I performed terribly in math in senior school, but I was excelling in my creative side, so I used to be picked up for important school activities. The music teacher would ask for me, and the art teacher would call me if something needed to be decorated. From fifth grade, it was evident to me that my creative side was dominating.

Pragya was also a badge-holder in school, and was selected as the house captain several times in her junior as well as her senior years. Pragya said that while she'd made multiple close best friends in school, she never felt the need to make friends in her neighbourhood. In fact, most of her after-school hours were either spent playing with her cousins or cycling on the Kamala Nehru Ridge (located near her house in Civil Lines). She also loved swimming. During this time, Pragya was inspired by her cousin Unnati, who is about four years her elder, to study different aspects of painting. Unnati was already in a polytechnic college when Pragya was still in school and used to paint a lot. "I learnt from her subconsciously", she said.

Pragya became the President of the Art Club in class twelve. In fact, that was the first time the school created a faculty of art, disclosed Naren*ji*. In 2001, Pragya cleared her senior secondary with a first class. She was also awarded a distinction in Arts following the AISSC Exams that year by the then President of India, (Late) Dr. Abdul Kalam Azad.

RAY FLORET

(Youth)

In 2001, Pragya gained admission to the prestigious Delhi College of Art. She was ranked seventh (All India) in the three-step examination process. Just before joining the Delhi School of Arts, Pragya attended the orientation meeting at JMC College. She'd briefly toyed with the idea of pursuing psychology from JMC, but at the orientation that day, Pragya finally realised that she wanted to pursue Art and not Psychology. "She was very proud of getting admitted into Delhi College of Art," said Devashish. Pragya chose applied art instead of painting or sculpture. Her mother, Ila*ji*, inspired her to take up applied art as "it keeps one abreast with how the world works", and today, she is reaping the benefit of that decision.

Pragya was enjoying her first year and the freedom that came with the transition from school to college, and she would always finish her assignments on time. The HoD of the first-year art faculty remarked that if Pragya had actually worked on it, the result would have been incredible. Even the work she had submitted stood out among the portfolios submitted by other students. "Whatever I did, I did because I loved doing it and that continues till today", said Pragya. Apart from studies, she was involved in several college activities, especially related to music. She was part of the college band, and along with the other members of the band, would participate in college musical events and intercollege competitions as a vocalist. "I went to all the college fests and competitions. '*Aaj Jaane Ki Zidd Na Karo*' and '*Aao Huzoor*' were a couple of my songs that were always in demand". She said that during this time, she was still a bit confused about her career choice and, at one point, felt compelled to go to a tarot card reader. The only question she asked the tarot reader was what she should anticipate for her professional life: music or art.

Discovering her Entrepreneurial Spirit

While still in college, Pragya earned her first paycheck by completing a small creative project of making handcrafted gel candles for Diwali. Pragya said she wanted to buy a cell phone for herself, but her parents offered to give her their broken second-hand phone that was tied up with a rubber band as a part of their parenting process. "They didn't want to give things to me easily". Her mother got her an order to make 300 candles. Pragya grabbed the opportunity to earn some money to buy her phone. "I calculated how much all the materials will cost, and I hand-painted the candles with tribal art through the wee hours of the night and my mom helped me throughout". It earned her a profit of fifteen thousand rupees. A friend of Pragya's who was visiting Dubai got her the phone for twelve-and-a-half thousand rupees.

In college, Pragya got her first commissioned work for a six-by-six feet painting from her maternal uncle, Sanjay Jain, a sought-after interior designer based in Kolkata. "Since it would have been my first commission ever, he asked me to share a reference and then make it", she said. "I went to the college library and found a Picasso, photocopied it, and showed it to him. Originally painted in 1907, the painting was called 'Three Women'". After her uncle approved, Pragya ordered 3 panels of 6×2 feet each, and painted a triptych. It took her two months to complete the piece. Her sister, Anugya, mentioned how she would watch Pragya painting away late into the night while she would fall off to sleep. "It was a huge piece spread across the wall of our bedroom and she would be painting away all night", she said.

Pragya made fifteen thousand rupees by selling her first painting. That was only the beginning. Over the years, Pragya completed several other commissioned works for Sanjay*ji*'s various projects. "I do commissioned work for his projects even now", she said. "There's a hotel owned by the Haldiram group in Kolkata, where an entire floor is curated with my paintings". While she was enjoying her college life and the freedom that came with it, it also posed some challenges regarding her studies. She said she really struggled to memorise all the events in History of Art. Also, despite being from a privileged background, her pocket money wasn't enough, so she learned to earn money on her own. "I learnt how every bit counts. I learnt management too, which is very important for an arts student", she said.

Finding Support

In 2005, Pragya graduated from college. Devashish recalled how his sister continued to be unsure of taking up graphic design as a career and was more inclined towards painting and creating her collections and finding her style. He said:

> I remember she showed me one of her college projects, it was a portrait she had made which was extremely detailed and very exquisite, it was made with just dots and no lines or brushwork. I encouraged her to continue to pursue more art, and she ended up making me three paintings in black-and-white monochromes. I still have them. They are geometrical black and white paintings that I have carried from house to house for over 20 years.

Pragya herself mentioned that her brother was a "huge driving force" in her feeling confident as an artist, and in life. Soon after her graduation, in the same year, Pragya displayed her first painting publicly at the Polka Art Gallery, New Delhi. It was a group exhibition. With encouragement and ample support from her family, Pragya started taking a serious interest in her work and began developing as an artist. "She had a very encouraging group of people around her that supported her, which was a plus", said Devashish.

Finding Love in Unexpected Ways

Pragya was still finding a footing in the art world when a major life change initiated a new chapter in her life. She had gotten engaged to Abhishek Jain towards the end of her last year of college, and in November 2005, they tied the knot. "We met only out of respect for our respective grandmoms who were friends. I was upset at first with my parents for thinking of marriage so early in life, but my parents said they wouldn't force me and would respect my decision after meeting Abhishek. He came from the US for a wedding and then travelled to Delhi to meet my family".

Abhishek describes the first time he met Pragya as one of his favourite memories. "Neither of us wanted to get hitched at that age, and we had a foolproof plan of fooling everyone...

but instead we became the fools who rushed into marriage", he said. "Pragya's confidence and the absolute happy-forever-vibe is what makes her who she is. That's who she was when I met her...I was hooked to this beautiful artsy gal. A rare and exquisite combination".

After nine months of courtship, in November that year, the two got married. Soon after their marriage, the couple shifted to Boston. Pragya said that even after shifting to the US, she continued to paint and exhibit her paintings in different art shows in New York City, Amherst, Boston, and several cities in Connecticut. "The first shopping I did in the US was for my art-supplies", she said. "I found my unique style in those initial months...I loved ballet and wanted to learn it when I was 12, but I was told I'm too old to start learning ballet at that age... It was something which stayed with me and maybe that's why I started painting ballerinas", she said. "I took hours to make shades and tones".

New Roots

Apart from discovering her own style as an artist, US life brought a big transition in her personality in many other ways. It was Abhishek who encouraged her to do little things by herself and built her confidence in a new country. With her husband's encouragement and her own determination to do things independently, she learnt the ways of her new life. "I've become a people's person in the US", she said. The couple also bought a house in Springfield in 2008. Abhishek said that he was always a fan of his wife's talent, and soon after their marriage, he got involved with her in exploring opportunities for her in the US. He said he bought the house as his first wedding gift to her, and it included an art studio of her own. "She created more than 40 artworks out of her studio in the span of a year, and was one of the founding members of the Women's Caucus for Art Association in Pioneer Valley, an organization which sprouts out of New York and has many artist members across the United States." Pragya became an influential artist and was doing shows all across the country, said Abhishek. Meanwhile, her brother Devashish, who was already settled in the US, began helping his sister as well in her artistic endeavours:

> I did two art shows in New York City, and I showed her paintings, and they sold! I think that might've given her a lot more confidence in her abilities. She also got a commission out of that show. She was very proud of it as those pieces are in or around New York, and since then, a collector in New York has commissioned, I think, about 7 to 8 paintings from her, which has been another boost in her portfolio.

FULL BLOOM

(Present)

In March 2008, Pragya's father, Naren*ji,* opened his own art gallery in Delhi, called the Art Mall. Pragya's paintings were showcased at their first group exhibition, along with those of other well-known artists. The exhibition was well received, and Pragya's paintings were greatly appreciated, increasing her popularity. After that, she did more shows with Art Mall, several shows in India, Bangladesh, Russia, and the US, disclosed Naren*ji*.

However, Pragya's big break came in 2009, when she held her first solo exhibition in Sublime Galleria, UB City, Bangalore. The seed for the solo exhibition of her paintings was sown much earlier. Uzma Irfan, a family friend (and the founder of Sublime Galleria), was visiting them in the summer of 2009. They galloped all around New York City, enjoying the day and talking about how life was in the US for her. During that time, the two friends got talking about Pragya's paintings. Pragya recalls:

> She returned to India, conceptualized a gallery, and called me saying, "You're our first artist, bring your art in November, we will have your Solo here, and I would be the happiest to promote you as my first artist at Sublime." The gallery opened in 2009 with my collection in a show titled 'Silhouettes'. The show was sold out. It was covered

> by every newspaper in Bangalore for several days. I woke up to find my photos in all magazines and newspapers every day. I was very grateful for this, and till today, I count my blessings for such a stellar start in India.

She went back to the US a few days after the show. However, after the huge success of her solo exhibition with Sublime, her association with them strengthened further, and she continues collaborating with the gallery. "Since then, I've had multiple solo and group shows with the gallery; the next one is in January 2024", she said.

Creating Opportunities for Herself

In 2011, Pragya and her husband decided to return to India. "My husband's job wasn't growing after a point. We took the active decision of selling the house and moving back to India, and we had a larger support system in India", she said. Pragya's parents-in-law (Mr. K.C. Jain & Mrs. Sunita Jain, renowned mining industrialists from the Misrilal Jain family of Kolkata) were settled in Bangalore along with her younger brother-in-law, who got married the same year. The couple shifted into the same house Abhishek grew up in after their return from the US.

Within a year of their return, Pragya became pregnant with her first child. It was during this time that she conceptualized her eco-conscious homeware label, Artychoke, over a phone conversation with her lawyer sister Anugya, who'd also recently relocated to Delhi from Mumbai. Anugya shared how the whole idea for Artychoke was formed. "I wanted to get into the home space, and she wanted to start making her art more accessible by creating products with her art...we started talking about our ideas, and that's how Artychoke was born". After some time, their mother, Ila*ji,* also joined the company, as she was a very strong driving force in the field of manufacturing.

The first set of products that were brought out under her label were pashmina shawls and cushion covers, with original designs by Pragya. "I always wanted to turn my art into beautiful things. I wanted to reach more and more homes with my creativity", said Pragya. By 2013, they had their own factory in Delhi and had expanded from two products to over a hundred products, including home décor and furniture. They were selling through their website. The work was well distributed between the two sisters and their mother from the very beginning. While Pragya creates the designs for Artychoke, Anugya handles the e–commerce business, and Ila*ji* takes care of the production.

Their first physical store was opened in Moti Nagar, Shivaji Marg, West Delhi, in 2015. As a new mom, starting a new business was a big challenge, but Pragya received ample support from her family and was able to manage both her roles well. "I established my brand Artychoke across India. I travelled when I could. My family has been a huge support. I received nothing but encouragement", she said. During this period, her husband Abhishek also started his own business. He co-founded his company, Terapact, which provides quality services in real estate marketing, brand marketing, marketing consulting, 3D design and more. While his own business required his time and attention, he supported his wife fully in her entrepreneurial journey. "We base our relationship on equality. He changed as many diapers as I did and stayed up as many nights as I did, and helped me with parenting duties". He's also been her soundboard (along with her sister and mother) and loves to critique her work, she said.

Finding Joy during the Pandemic

Apart from painting and managing her label, during the Covid lockdown, Pragya also took to teaching art. She started online classes for kids in the summer of 2020, when the pandemic was at its peak. "I started with kids, but now I also teach adults", she said. "My motive was interaction. Covid lockdown was a depressive phase, so online classes were my escape. I had always been approached by parents to teach art to their kids. Within a couple of days of sharing the flyer about my online classes, we had registered about 12–15 kids from different parts of India and even from other countries". She said teaching art gives her joy, and one of her goals is to open an art school. It was also during the lockdown that she got to spend more time with her little son, Arhaan. "I like to hang around him even if he's just sketching, making lego, or playing his guitar", she said.

In January 2023, Pragya gave birth to her daughter Inaaya. With a wide gap of 10 years between her two kids, she has loved every bit of watching Inaaya grow. While Pragya is busy playing different roles, her love for painting continues, and she says she creates a balance between her artistic and entrepreneurial needs. "I have a studio at home, and I like to work on my paintings at night, as during the day, I have to run my company and create designs for my products". While Pragya is a gallery artist, many of her paintings are also displayed in her stores. Apart from their e–commerce business, they have successfully managed to open physical stores of Artychoke, from one in Moti Nagar (West Delhi), which was opened in 2015, to a store in Emami Art Gallery (Kolkata), a shop in Ffolio (Bangalore), and earlier this year they inaugurated their newest store which is in the well-known UB city mall in Vittal Mallya Road (Bangalore).

Being an artist and an entrepreneur comes naturally to Pragya. She articulates it beautifully:

> I come from a business family. I married into a business family. I want my paintings to reach more homes. My main goal is to communicate through colours, and I am forever fascinated by the human experience. I spend hours finding perfect symmetry on my canvas, adding layer upon layer to achieve geometric perfection. It signifies our desire to find comfort in repetition, routine, and structure. This is what I believe to be a direct representation of what the human mind wants and acts like. Ultimately, I wish that my creations exude positivity and happiness. This vision inspired the eco-conscious homeware label Artychoke. We are constantly creating pieces that can fit into every aspect of everyday life. I find a beautiful irony in how I have created the perfect symmetry in my role as an artist and a designer—one cannot live without the other.

9

Preeti Das

Stand-up Comedian, Actor & Academician

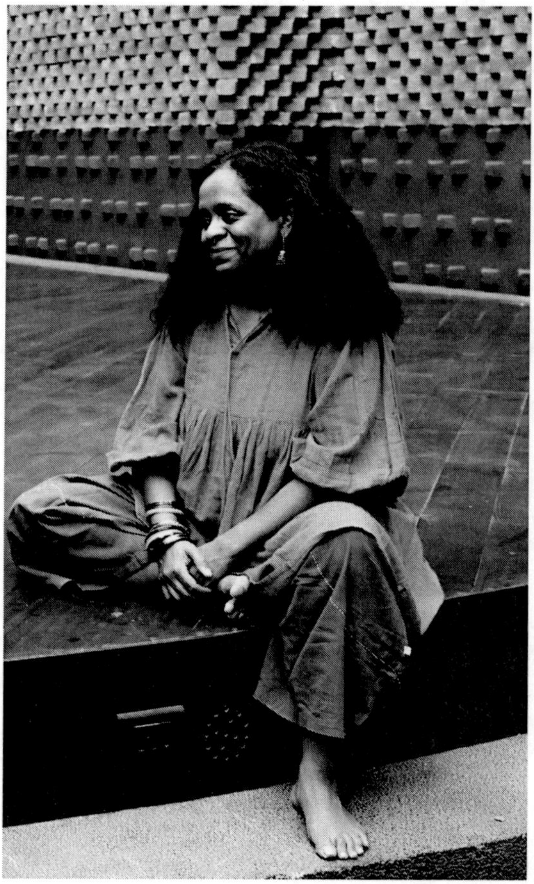

Figure 9

"I've always been a funny person from the beginning, with presence of mind and a little craziness. Stand-up comedy has to be accessible (to all). It shouldn't be limited to pubs and nightclubs."

—Preeti Das

PREETI DAS (b. 1970) is the first female stand-up comedian in Gujarat. She has been doing stand-up comedy for over 12 years now. An award-winning journalist, Preeti won the Ladlee Media Award for Investigative Journalism in India (first in the Western zone and then in Asia) in 2015–16 for her series of stories on gang-rape victims. She has over 20 years of work experience, which includes being a former journalist with Aaj Tak, Indian Express and DNA, heading the communication team at ActionAid International's Tsunami Project, a radio jockey with Radio Mirchi, additional director at Karnavati University's Department of Mass Communication and Liberal Arts and a qualitative market researcher. Currently, she teaches a course titled "The Art of Storytelling and Performance" at Ahmedabad University.

As a stand-up comedian, she has performed at the Mathrubhumi International Literature Festival (MBIFL), Gujarat Literature Festival (GLF), Natarani Amphitheater, Round Table India charity event, Vir Das' Pyjama Festival, United Nations celebration of the International Day of the Girl Child, CRY's event on Child Rights and One Million Rising to name a few. She regularly performs at various venues across India.

She is the co-founder of Mahila Manch, an all-women stand-up comedy collective that works on a host of issues still considered taboo in our society. Preeti has worked with various organizations, and trains women to use stand-up comedy to talk about issues that include domestic violence, reproduction rights, menstrual issues, and child marriages.

Preeti's scripts and sets are edgy, bold, and honest. She believes in using comedy for awareness and advocacy.

STARBUD

(Childhood)

Preeti was born in Cuddalore, an ancient historic district of Tamil Nadu. Her (late) mother, Vijayalakshmi Das, was a Tamilian, while her father, Dr. Biswaswaroop Das, is a Bengali. The couple met in Ahmedabad while studying Urban Planning, fell in love, and got married at a young age. They started their married life in Surat, but since it was a small town that had few job opportunities for Vijaylaxmi*ji*, she decided to move to Ahmedabad with both her daughters, Preeti and Swati (who is four years younger), while her husband continued to work in Surat. Both girls were born in Cuddalore in their grandparents' home, and were raised by them for the first couple of years of their childhood.

Preeti's first memories of childhood are of wearing her *Patti's* (Grandmother's) cotton sari. She also recalled how *Patti* would tell her stories only in Tamil so that she could pick up the language. The knowledge of Tamil later helped Preeti in her first job as a TV journalist in Aaj Tak, Chennai. Dr. Das described his daughter as someone who was always an outgoing girl and "loved to eat, particularly fish". He also mentioned how Preeti started talking very early, when she was around a year and a half. He said one of his linguist friends found it amazing that at three years of age, Preeti could construct short sentences. She liked to play with mud and sand, and "was always found outside the house rather than inside", he said. Preeti was around five when she first performed on stage in Surat, playing the role of a strict teacher.

Preeti's grandparents continued to be a strong support to her working parents, and took care of both the girls even afterwards. While their grandmother passed away when the girls were still young, their grandfather came to live with them in Ahmedabad, and took responsibility for them as their mom had a full-time job. Their father, Dr. Das, would visit the family only on weekends, and Preeti said she looked forward to his visits. He not only brought gifts for both the girls, but his visits also meant two days of fun activities and outings. In Ahmedabad,

Preeti and her sister were admitted to an all-girls convent school, Mt. Carmel. "We were brought up by the strictest of nuns", Preeti said.

In school, she was an above-average student. She wasn't a rank-holder, but she did well in academics. Moreover, there was no pressure from her parents to get top scores. "I enjoyed school and I used to read a lot of books like *The Mallory Towers* series and other books by Enid Blyton, and slowly graduated to the Sydney Sheldon kind of books". When Preeti was in class eight, their school organized a visit to an all-boys school, and Preeti said there was a lot of excitement around it. Now, when she talks about sexuality and reproductive health through her performances, she says she brings her reflections and her responses from that phase of hers into these shows.

One of her closest school friends, Kanchan, was a tomboy whom Preeti first met in class eight. "Kanchan came during the mid-term and she was different. She looked like a rebel. We hit it off immediately", said Preeti. The two continued to be best friends till college, when they had to choose different streams. Finally, after college, Kanchan shifted to Pune, and Preeti left for Chennai to pursue her master's. Another good friend with whom she spent a good amount of time during her childhood was Harpreet. They used to go cycling and jogging together. Participating in extra-curricular activities like school plays and elocution competitions came naturally to Preeti, and she won many awards in elocution competitions. "They (both the girls) had the freedom to do whatever they loved. The freedom came by default and by design", said Dr. Das.

Her younger sister, Swati, who was in the same school as Preeti, described her sister as being "extremely active in all kinds of extra-curricular activities".

Facing Discrimination

Every year during Christmas, the school organized plays in which Preeti was made the King every time. Once, in the middle of a play, she stopped and confronted her teacher and asked her why she was not given other characters to play. She said her teacher told her that only fair girls would be given other roles.

Preeti went back home crying that day at the unfairness of it all. "My complexes around my skin started from there", she said.

Another incident she narrated was of a classmate, Jonita—also dark-skinned—who was insulted by a teacher during their stitching class with the rude comment, "Your cloth is as ugly as your face". Preeti said these discriminations damaged her emotionally. She uses these past reflections in her humourous stories to make a point on topics like colour bias, gender discrimination and other women-centric issues. "The word black gets to me...I've been dented at a tender age by my friends, teachers and even girls at the beauty parlours...that was the first time I started being rebellious and challenging stereotypes", she said. "I was also slightly plump, so they used to call me '*kali*' or '*moti*'". These complexes prompted Preeti to get into an extreme fitness regime, and she even started dieting when she was still very young. In fact, her father, she said, would often scold her and ask her not to overdo things. Preeti also learnt Bharatnatyam for four years during her school years in order to lose weight.

Many such incidents from her past later acted as the trigger for some of her stand-up shows, where she used them to expose the flaws of society using humour and satire.

Dealing with Loss

Preeti was extremely close to her mother—who, at that time, was working with Aga Khan Rural Support Program (AKRSP) in Ahmedabad—and she would often miss school to accompany her mother on her field visits or at times land up at her mom's office after school and spend time with her while she worked. "She loved reading with me, and she loved travelling with her mother", Dr. Das said.

Her mom's sudden passing away a few years ago came as a huge jolt to Preeti. "She was a fantastic mum. She was always there for the PTMs and was a great cook", Preeti said. "A lot of my comfort around rural journalism comes from her. She always believed that women must be independent. When she passed away, the kind of people that came for her funeral were amazing". Preeti is quite close to her younger sister, Swati, who is a film and theatre actor. However, the two refrain from talking about their mother after her death. It is too painful for them. In fact, Preeti still addresses her mother in the present tense.

Swati said that her sister had the chance to spend a lot more time with Amma than she had since she moved out of home and lived in hostels after she finished her schooling. "Preeti, who is in general very particular about celebrating important events of life, was mostly the one who would take charge when it came to Amma's birthday, or anniversary, or any other important event. Buying gifts, writing on cards, organising dinners, etcetera, was generally done by Preeti", she said.

Preeti took up commerce in class twelve, but said she didn't enjoy it as much. However, she passed her senior secondary exams with decent scores. "School left me with a few complexes about the way I am", she said.

RAY FLORET

(Youth)

In 1997, Preeti got admission to St. Xavier's, Ahmedabad. She changed her stream to Economics (Honours) as she loved the subject. She said it was a wonderful period. "...a lot of me was shaped in college. I was a naughty girl with the gift of gab. I was doing dance, theatre, choreography, classical and semi-classical dance. I was all over the place".

Preeti's teachers in college instilled in her the "idea of equality". This put her at ease. "I suddenly got exposed to people from the Northeast and different communities. Even my seniors were good to us". The open and vibrant environment of her college had a positive effect on her personality. No one made fun of her skin colour. In fact, she was called dusky, she revealed, "and they left it at that".

In her final year, she won the coveted title of "Miss Xavier" for her all-around achievements in academics and co-curricular activities. There were five to six candidates contesting for the title. The final rounds were tough, and one of the adjudicators was from outside the college. Preeti cleared all the rounds decisively and was declared a winner. One of Preeti's college juniors (and a friend), who is a popular RJ with Radio Mirchi, Ahmedabad, Devaki Marcus, described her as "spontaneous, high on energy and life". "She's unabashed about things she believes in, and she doesn't filter her thoughts", Devaki said.

Preeti was quite popular from her first year onwards and made plenty of friends. She continues to be in touch with many of them. "One of my college friends, Sikandar, is my lawyer. After my mom's death, there was so much paperwork, and Sikandar helped us", Preeti revealed. Her best friend from school, Kanchan, was also in the same college. The two friends met only during college fests as both had taken different streams. Preeti said college life was very enjoyable for her.

In 2000, freshly out of college, Preeti joined SEWA, Ahmedabad. "They were setting up SEWA Insurance and so I did a little study for them", she said. In 2001, the Bhuj earthquake happened. Her father's friend called to say that they needed volunteers to collect the list of names of missing persons. Brijesh Kumar Singh (Zee TV) was then the senior journalist in the control room handling the entire operation, and Preeti worked under him. She said that every evening after finishing work, he would tell her things she found interesting. In the same year, she joined Manipal, Karnataka, to pursue her master's in Mass Communication. "I did it without thinking", she said. "I wanted to be a TV reporter".

She said that while the course was rigorous, she had a great time there and picked up critical thinking skills while doing the course. She also met her best friend, Yamini Karthik, there. Yamini was her roommate, and they hit it off almost immediately. "Two years were focused and there was freedom", said Preeti. "I did my internship with Sun TV and stayed at Yamini's house". Yamini said Preeti was the opposite of her in nature, and yet they hit it off from the moment they met. "Preeti was always the life of the party and a force to reckon with", she said. "We had a lot of crazy adventures in Manipal". She recounted a hilarious incident from the time both friends were invited as chief guests to inaugurate a beauty shop outside Manipal that only had men in the audience. When it was time for them to speak, she said, Preeti just stood up and spoke about inner beauty, using humour to convey the message. "It was funny and really nice", she said.

Engaging in Meaningful Work

After completing her course from Manipal, Preeti joined Aaj Tak. "They took me immediately because I could speak both Hindi and Tamil. They were frantically looking for someone like me. I was with them for a few years. I covered arts, culture, and politics, but the turning point for me was on 26 December 2004, when the deadly Tsunami struck Marina Beach". She said she and her sister had gone out for dinner the night before, and her uncle had called her from Andaman to inform her of a strong earthquake they had experienced. The next morning, it had hit the shores of Chennai, including Marina Beach.

"Immediately nothing happened. We went to Marina Beach. A cameraman came along. It was a Sunday morning and soon Marina Beach was inundated with water, and there was chaos everywhere. There was water everywhere. I was going from one mortuary to the other. I was reporting in Hindi. There was a lot of crying...I saw a pretty girl dead". This experience shook her and left a lasting impression on her. "The Tsunami trauma stayed with me", she said. Preeti worked on some other high-profile cases, including the "Sankararaman Murder Case" in September 2004. "It was an eye-opener for a young woman like me". During this phase, she experienced high stress due to the nature of her work. "Covering other news became traumatic", she said. In 2005, she decided to leave Aaj Tak, and returned home to Ahmedabad.

Once home, she took time off to figure out whether she wanted to work or study. At that time, ActionAid was looking for someone to steer their Tsunami Response Programme in India and Sri Lanka. Preeti joined them as their Head of Communications. It involved a lot of travel to Tamil Nadu, Andaman, and she even lived in Sri Lanka for six months covering stories. A disaster of such magnitude and its aftermath had to be documented, and the stories needed to be brought out. "People who were being rehabilitated had a lot of stories with them. We went to the remotest of fishing colonies", said Preeti. She recorded the stories while monitoring the fund disbursement and overseeing the project. Once the mega-project was over, Preeti left ActionAid and soon joined a marketing research agency in Bangalore, involving a lot of communication and travel as well. "I was enjoying myself. I did a lot of fieldwork because I knew so many languages. I used to do group discussions in Tamil, Bengali, Gujarati, English and Hindi. People would come to watch my Focused Group Discussions. My exercises were fun". Preeti worked with them for a little under three years, and during this time, she was sharing a flat with her good friend Yamini, who was also working in Bangalore.

FULL BLOOM

(Present)

In 2010, Preeti left her job in Bangalore to return home once again. The man she loved had ditched her just "at the last moment". Preeti didn't know what she would do in Ahmedabad, but she needed time to heal from her broken relationship. She decided it was best to be with her parents. It was during this time that a good friend, Ajit Pal Singh, who was organizing the Ahmedabad Film Festival, approached her to join him and help him out with curating the festival.

Joining the film festival team not only helped Preeti take her mind off the pain of a broken heart, but she also met her husband Jay Thakkar, an academician and a film buff, for the first time. While Preeti's job was to take care of the film festival panels and ensure that the sessions were conducted smoothly, Jay was there as a juror. He was running late by a few minutes for his session, and since Preeti was coordinating his panel, Jay messaged her to let her know that he was running "four minutes late". Preeti responded to his message with a smiley emoji. "When I went there, she was kind of laughing that 'four minutes late…?' Now, after all these years, I understand why she was laughing…because wherever we go, she's nearly forty minutes late". During the panel discussion, Jay also asked why there were no women on the panel. His thoughtful remarks again impressed Preeti.

The two were drawn to each other immediately. "She was loud, witty, humorous, and beautiful. She had dark skin, permed hair, and was full of energy. The best part about her was her smile. She was very gorgeous. She's still gorgeous", Jay said, sharing his first impressions of Preeti and what drew him towards her. The two started dating each other soon after they met, and in December 2010, they married. "We're diagrammatically opposite in many ways...we used to call each other yin-yang. We were different in terms of food, culture, our interests...but what bound us together were our deep core values of life: what we believe in, what is important, and how we see society".

Realising her Creative Potential

After the film festival, Preeti decided to work full-time again and went to Radio Mirchi's office. They were looking for someone for their show, *Purani Jeans*, dedicated to nostalgic music. Preeti did her mic test and landed the job as an RJ. "I worked with them for 11 months. I did so many lovely interviews with Bappi Lahiri, Shammi Kapoor, Usha Uthup, and so many others". Around the same time, she joined Karnavati University's Department of Mass Communication and Liberal Arts as their Associate Director, and started teaching. However, the turning point in her artistic life came when she met Mannan, an RJ in Baroda. "He'd left Radio Mirchi and joined My FM, and that was the time he was starting to experiment with stand-up. I asked him, "why do you have only men in your show?" Mannan, in response, asked Preeti to join them.

Preeti did her first stand-up comedy set in Baroda in 2011. In fact, that year, she hosted a couple of shows. "I used to be the only woman". In 2012, she got pregnant with her son, but continued for the initial months before taking a maternity break. "When my son was three months old, I started doing it again", she said. She would breastfeed her son and go to her shows. She said it wasn't easy as there was no space for new moms to feed their infants, and she had to struggle with it for some time. She later did a stand-up set on breastfeeding mothers and their challenges. Preeti dotes on her son and is an extremely engaged parent, and Jay describes Preeti as a "tigress" when it comes to being a mother. "Her life essentially revolves around Kabir. Her own decisions in life revolve around Kabir", he said. Devaki, too, said that Preeti's "bond with her kid and her husband is amazing".

By 2012, she had started doing stand-up full-time. However, she continued to be drawn towards journalism. DNA was looking for a health reporter, and Preeti interviewed and got the job. She became a reporter during the week and a stand-up artist on weekends. "If DNA had not closed down, I would be with them even now", said Preeti. Preeti's ex-boss in DNA, Shyam Parekh, was full of praise for his ex-colleague. "Preeti is a wonderful person, an infectious bundle of creative energy who livens up the space she's in". He went on to add that "she's committed to journalism in its true essence, and showed exemplary courage in chasing stories that needed to be told, even risking herself without blinking an eyelid".

However, it was through stand-up and theatre that Preeti creatively presented the stories she encountered using humour and satire. In that sense, both her professions were complementary to each other, and that was also the reason that the flavours of her stand-up shows are so different. "I was covering serious issues. I started taking my own stories and turned them into stand-up. I did a story on contraception. I was reporting on a sexual harassment case, later, spinning it into a stand-up. I thought it was a powerful tool of communication".

However, she accepted that it wasn't easy for her. While she became popular in Ahmedabad and was invited to several prestigious festivals around the country to perform, she had to struggle hard to keep her footing and be visible in her chosen field. As a woman stand-up artist talking about censored topics, Preeti had to face several unpleasant experiences, especially during private gigs. At times, she had to cut her shows short due to unruly crowds. "It's still a boys' club and even the audience is male in majority". In December 2017, Preeti founded the Mahila Manch along with Shefali Pandey. Mahila Manch is a platform for women and other underrepresented groups, where they can be heard and seen. The collective has gained popularity for engaging with contemporary issues in politics, gender, and identity. "Under Mahila Manch, we did shows on completely taboo topics. We did a show with women bootleggers and called it 'Bewada Gujarat'. It was all sold out. We also did a show with Asha Workers. I trained the Asha workers on how to do stand-up comedy". She said that while most Gujaratis are business-minded, they're progressive as a society and welcomed and appreciated her shows.

Preeti believes that stand-up comedy is for everyone. "Let's give everyone an opportunity to tell their stories, especially those from underprivileged backgrounds. So we, through Mahila Manch, give everyone—the LGBTQ, women, Asha Workers, bootleggers—that platform to tell their stories". Preeti's shows also address all age groups. In fact, she's increasingly focusing on children now. She's spontaneous on stage, and decides what kind of jokes will work after seeing the audience. This ability to quickly change and adapt according to the environment and the collective mood is what she's good at. The well-known Ahmedabad-based singer, Aishwarya Joshi, who has been working with Preeti on a project and is also a good friend, said, "Crazy is the word for Preeti. She's the naughtiest woman I've met. She can do anything because she's fearless. She speaks her heart and mind. She isn't afraid of anyone or anything. A woman I look up to".

From a TV reporter, to a radio jockey and a print journalist, academician, and finally to being Gujarat's first woman stand-up artist, Preeti has worn different hats, making an impact wherever she has worked.

She continues to do what she loves best, and is good at making people laugh while gently nudging them to ponder on serious issues. She's also teaching a course titled "The Art of Storytelling and Performance" at Ahmedabad University.

As her father, Dr. Das, puts it: "Her latent desire was always to be on stage. During all the jobs she was doing, she continued with her stand-up. She doesn't get bored of the stage and she'll continue...she seems to be enjoying it".

10
Shilpika Bordoloi

Dancer, Filmmaker, Educator & Curator

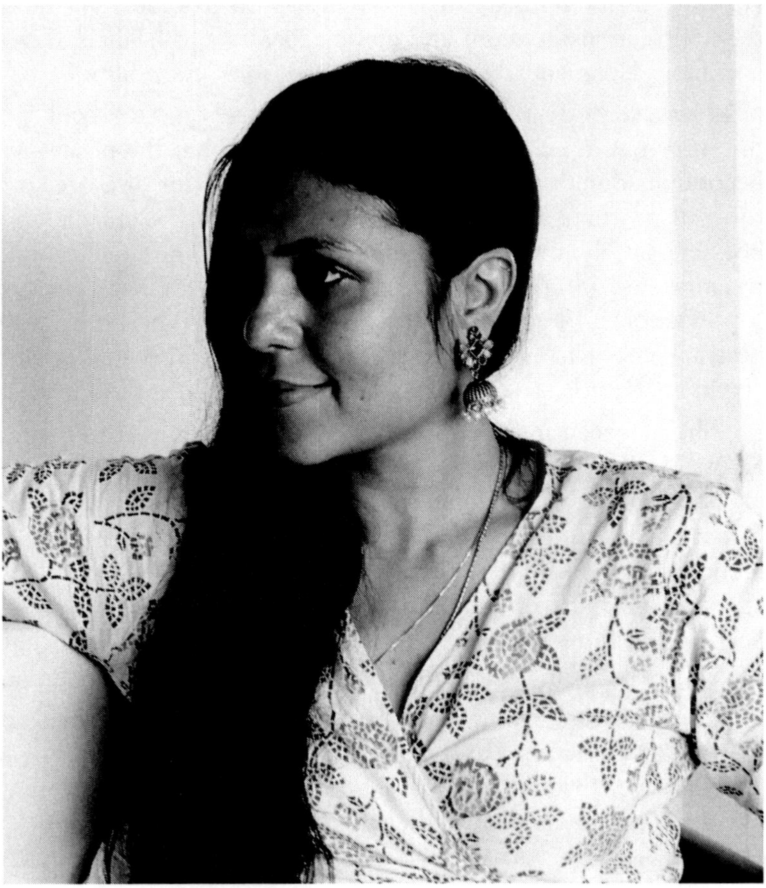

Figure 10

"Pause is so important. In all my compositions I need that silence, that pause."

—Shilpika Bordoloi

SHILPIKA BORDOLOI (b. 1981) is a multidisciplinary artist working with movement/dance, theatre, film, community and healing practices. She is the founder/artistic director of Brahmaputra Cultural Foundation, a space of—and for—community participation, leadership, artistic journeys/performances, and education through a sync of ancestral wisdom, indigenous knowledge systems, and modernity. Currently, her approach broadly subsumes the intersections between and among theatre and healing, dance and film, dance and theatre, fiction and non-fiction film.

Her exercises and techniques are based on 'stop-look-go' or 'entry-pause-exit' principles. She believes that the process of becoming something is internal and requires a lot of correction too—of postures and methods practised—and that shift is only possible slowly, by observing and accepting. While her healing practices aid in creating transparency in life, for her, it is not a philosophical condition but a physical one. The body must be transparent to be able to let in the light, air, water or fire, elephant, tree. It is necessary so that the audience feels it too.

She has been involved in an extraordinary range of pursuits across diverse platforms. Several of her endeavours have focused on issues affecting her community, including the environment/climate crisis and the people. She is a visiting faculty at the National School of Drama and National Institute of Design, and at State University of Film and Television, Haryana. Shilpika has been awarded the Sangeet Natak Akademi Ustad Bismillah Khan Yuva Puraskar for Contemporary/Experimental Dance in India.

She is also a Yoga Teacher (*Siromani*). She facilitates healing workshops for women and men for empowerment, nourishment and balance, through modules, both individual and collective, live and online. Currently, she is exploring the broad umbrella of Body Wisdom, where healing modalities, film, performance, and community work come together.

STARBUD

(Childhood)

Shilpika Bordoloi was born in Jorhat, a culturally rich and important urban centre of Assam. Her parents, Girish Chandra Bordoloi, an Executive Engineer with PWD, and Sabitri Bordoloi, a housewife, teacher and musician, were both animal lovers. Consequently, Shilpika, along with her two brothers, grew up with different kinds of animals at home as pets. "My father had a special relationship with animals. One of our favourite stories to hear was about his experiences when he had a bear cub, a dog, and a python living with him. At some point at home, we were three kids, a turtle, a parrot, three dogs, poultry and around eighteen cows", said Shilpika. She said her parents encouraged the three siblings to have a close relationship with nature. "When fresh hay would be delivered for the cows, we loved to play in the haystack. Mom would oil us up and we would spend the entire day there". When the kids fell sick, medicines were from the kitchen garden instead of allopathy, a practice Shilpika continues to follow till date.

Her first prominent childhood memory is of her great-grandmother passing away. She was barely three. She vividly recalled how she'd cried seeing her great-grandmother in her last minutes while her dad held her in his arms. This memory would later spark many conversations of memory, maternal inter-generational multi-sensory experiences as an artist, and also endless stories on the fascinating life of her great grandmother, freedom fighter Purbeshwari Doloi.

Shilpika's elder brother, Gautam (who is two and a half years older than her), was her childhood hero. She said her aim in life was to be like her brother. "I was a massive follower of my brother. I only wanted to wear clothes that he wore. And I kept short hair just like him. I also wanted his toys, and threw all the dolls away. He would let me play". When Gautam started school, she also would dress up in the same school uniform and attend a pre-school and then would wait for him to finish his classes and return home. When she started school, her parents had to get special permission to allow her to wear the boys' uniform in school.

Her childhood was busy but a happy one, she said. Her younger brother, Rupam, was five years younger than her, and much like Gautam was Shilpika's hero, Rupam's role model was his older sister. He followed the same pattern and insisted on dressing up like her and followed her around. The three siblings were close to each other and had the most fun in the house, while both her parents would go out in the evenings, leaving them to study. Shilpika was an exceptional student and did well in extra-curricular activities as well. She changed schools twice. She was first admitted to a school owned by family friends called HHMI. She recalls one of her childhood memories:

> One of my strongest memories from childhood is from class three. We had our art class. We were all asked to draw a lotus flower. I was pretty good at art and drew the lotus well. However, my benchmate was given 9/10 by the teacher, while I got 3/10. I went up to the art teacher and asked him why he had given me lower marks even when my drawing was better than my classmate's. I showed the sheet to the principal and asked for more marks. I stood up for what I thought was wrong. It came from within me.

In class four, her parents admitted her to Carmel, a co-ed school in Jorhat. It wasn't an easy transition for her. She felt she was being judged for everything in her new school, and she became "a bit of an introvert". "I couldn't articulate my feelings to my parents...and the whole expectation was to excel", she said. "I was pampered by my dad, but mom was strict with all of us". Since Shilpika was a bright child, she did well in her studies.

Her First Tryst with Dance

She started learning Manipuri dance at the age of three, and her first public performance was when she was about five. It was her mother who initiated her into dancing by engaging a teacher for her at home. "My mother was fascinated by dance, and I think she wanted Shilpika to learn", said Gautam, her older brother. "Shilpika was around three when the dance teacher came to our house...by the age of five, she was already being taken out for performances".

However, it wasn't so easy for Sabitri*ji* to get her daughter to agree to attend the dance classes. It was Gautam who'd come to the rescue. Sabitri*ji* decided to get her son to attend the dance classes with her daughter. Seeing her brother taking classes with her, little Shilpika started taking an interest in dancing. Her dance teacher, (Late) Guru Rathindra Sinha was actually a Pung player, but knew the traditional drum of the Manipuri Meitei community. He taught her dance performance and developed in her a love and passion for dancing. "My relationship with dance happened because of him", said Shilpika. She said she learnt the right technique much later when (in her twenties) she got a chance to be under the tutelage of the famous Jhaveri sisters, leading exponents of the Manipuri dance form in Mumbai.

A Mixed Bag of Experiences

In school, Shilpika was popular not only because she was good at dance but also because she excelled in her studies. One of her closest childhood friends, Vikramjit Barua, said, "She was intelligent, good-looking, and multitalented. Moreover, she always had an artistic and creative streak, be it different forms of dance, painting, or organising and performing on stage". Yet, despite her talent and popularity, Shilpika continued to face problems articulating her thoughts and feelings to others as she felt people around her judged her and had too many expectations from her.

During a school competition for which Shilpika had to travel to another school with other students, she got her period for the second time. Her friend Shahida, who was a year older, enlightened her about the menstrual cycle and sexual intercourse. Shilpika was in class seven at that time. She said that while she'd been receiving a lot of attention from boys from class two onwards, and had curiosities, she hadn't openly talked about the changes in her body with anyone before her conversation with Shahida on the bus that day. She'd been glad and thankful to her friend for educating her about a subject she knew very little about.

Alternate Modes of Educating Herself

During her childhood, Shilpika was also greatly influenced by her grandparents, especially her maternal grandfather. "In my view, from her childhood, because she lived close to our house, she was close to me and my husband", said Bhabani*ji*, Shilpika's ninety-year-old maternal grandmother. "She loved us and since she was a kid, she listened to us". Shilpika's grandfather, (Late) Debeswar Doloi was a freedom fighter and told her stories of the freedom struggle and his time spent in jail. The understanding of the idea of freedom was important to her. She said she would have long discussions with him on socio-political issues and what freedom meant to him. He talked of independence of all kinds, including the freedom to choose, to take decisions, and having an independent worldview. She feels she's imbibed these traits from him.

"Education is something I'm passionate about. Certificates are nothing. They don't mean anything. I've learnt much from my grandparents", she said. Her paternal grandmother was a fierce matriarch, and her ways of discipline and expression of love had an influence on her emerging philosophies. The older she got, the more valuable they were in reflection.

RAY FLORET

(Youth)

After completing her senior secondary schooling from Cotton College, Guwahati, in 1999, Shilpika took admission in Lady Shri Ram (LSR) College, Delhi, for her graduation. Bhaabani*ji* recalled how she accompanied Shilpika's mom and Shilpika for admission in LSR, as her father could not travel due to his work. Getting into LSR wasn't easy. Shilpika wanted to study Psychology, but the subject of her choice was available at a different college. In LSR, she was offered English Literature and decided to take it up as she'd always wanted to get into the college. "From class seven, I had heard a lot about LSR and so I dreamt of it", she said. Shilpika continued to learn dance. In fact, in classes eleven and twelve, her mother made her join Bharatanatyam classes in Guwahati, but it was a slow learning, with classes happening only once a month, and more like a hobby. Her family thought Shilpika would either become an educationist or a bureaucrat. She, however, was "thoroughly confused" about what she wanted to do after her graduation.

College life was busy, and besides her studies, Shilpika actively participated in co-curricular activities like Spic Macay and the Dance Society Choreography team. Shilpika's good friend from college, Charu Shankar, whom she met in the first few weeks of joining college, had this to say about her friend and how she met her:

> Trials for the dance team were held for the first-year students, and the auditorium was packed with enthusiastic girls. Everyone wanted to prove their mettle; it was a great opportunity to be selected for the team. Not just me, everyone was mesmerised when a tall, slim, and beautiful girl with long hair came on stage and performed the most sublime, soft dance in such a powerfully delicate way! It left such a powerful impression in my memory, I can still see it so clearly, like it was yesterday!

Charu further added that what she found incredible about her friend was her earnestness, dedication to learning, and innate wisdom. "She's always been able to give me another perspective that I would have never thought of on my own".

A Delicate Balancing Act

Shilpika said she had little time to socialise during college. However, she wanted to keep dancing. She sought out her guru, the acclaimed Bharatnatyam dancer, Leela Samson (or Leela *Akka*, as she's fondly called by her disciples) and studied under her. "My parents helped me get in touch with Leela *Akka* through Subhalaxmi*ji* (Ustad Amjad Ali Khan's wife) and requested her to help me. I met Leela *Akka* in Subhalaxmi*ji*'s drawing room". Shilpika started learning Bharatnatyam under Leela*ji* soon after. She would attend college classes during the day, and learn Bharatnatyam in the evenings. "*Akka* had big expectations from me. She was sure I would become a Bharatnatyam dancer. She would make fish for me lovingly, but I was intimidated by her", said Shilpika.

Shilpika was also under much pressure from all sides. "My parents wanted me to do my master's in English Literature, and *Akka* wanted me to focus full time on dance", she said. She couldn't communicate her feelings to *Akka*. "She was expecting me to perform and preparing me for a dance event in China as part of her troupe, Spanda. But in my first year of M.A., I stopped going to her.

After many years I wrote a long letter to *Akka*, and said sorry. She replied by saying all the best and it ended there. We haven't crossed paths after that". Not going to *Akka's* Bharatnatyam classes was a turning point in her dance journey. She was in M.A. second year (2003) and had stopped dancing abruptly as she felt overwhelmed and unsure about it. Instead, she went to intern in corporate communication at Turner's CNN and Cartoon Network. She said she liked working there as she loved cartoons, and was working for the launch of POGO and creating creative activities based on Cartoon shows for kids. Her parents were happy that their daughter had finally started working with a prestigious corporate house. Yet, Shilpika was still unsure where she was heading.

A Turning Point

It was during this time that she learnt about *Kalarippayattu*, the traditional martial-arts form of Kerala. The form intrigued her, and she decided to find out more about it. While searching for a teacher who could teach her Kalari, Shilpika came to know about Daksha Sheth, who lived in Trivandrum. Shilpika got in touch with her via email. Daksha*ji* responded and asked Shilpika to come to Kerala. Shilpika decided to quit her cushy job in Delhi and also informed her parents of her move. Reluctantly, both her parents insisted on accompanying her to a village in Trivandrum, where Daksha Sheth and her Australian husband Dev Issro (a musician and a photographer) lived and practised contemporary dance.

Shilpika and her parents were put up at a cottage, close to their house, in the beautiful and secluded lakeside spot, with a forest next to it. There were eight other boys from Kerala, who were there to learn *Kalari* like her, but none of them spoke

English. After Shilpika's parents left, the couple's 10-year-old son Tao slept in the cottage with her for almost ten days as she was scared to be on her own in that house. However, slowly, she became comfortable in her new environment and started immersing herself in her idyllic life. "They were experimental people. Dada would take me to the lake for a swim. I helped Didi with the household chores, and learnt yoga. Basically, I was living with them. I soon realised I was enjoying this exploration of doing my own thing", she said. "I was in the midst of nature, away from people, swimming in the lake, and I could breathe. I took a pause. In all my compositions I need that silence, that pause".

In 2004, her teacher asked her to choreograph a small piece for their show. It was then that she realised how much she enjoyed dance and the whole process of creation. "Immediately after the show, Didi asked me to sign a contract with them". However, Shilpika was unsure due to parental pressure and decided to return to Mumbai. By the end of 2004, Shilpika was back in Mumbai. Here, she met Ranjana Jhaveri and Darshana Jhaveri, leading exponents of *Manipuri* classical dance and famously known as the "Jhaveri Sisters". Shilpika said they were good friends of Daksha*ji*. "I told them I love dance but wasn't clear about what is it in dance that I want to do". The Jhaveri sisters were "very welcoming" and took her under their wing. Darshana*ji* said of her pupil, "She had the typical grace for *Manipuri* and was soft-spoken and delicate, having a physique suitable for the stage. She showed keen interest, and we taught her and came close to each other". Classes would happen thrice a week.

During this time, Shilpika was also looking for a job. "I joined a PR company. I was staying with a friend, but I had to pay my rent. The PR company was taking a lot of my time, so I quit that and joined a publishing house as an editor". Learning dance from the Jhaveri sisters was a different experience for Shilpika. "They were adorable people. It was a different kind of relationship with them. I learnt *Manipuri* dance in their beautiful house facing the sea. And while we would be immersed in the class, the sea would also immerse me". However, Shilpika realised that while she loved *Manipuri*, it wasn't for her.

In 2005, she met her first husband, with whom she had a 7-month relationship, including marriage. He was a graphic comic writer who was practising street living. The marriage lasted less than two months, and divorce happened quickly. Her bad marriage took a toll on her. She returned to Assam. "I broke down…I came back home and didn't want to go back to Mumbai".

Exploring her Potential

In 2007, Shilpika relocated to Delhi with the conviction that she wanted to be a contemporary dancer. Gautam, her older brother, was already working in Delhi, and she shifted in with him. Not only was Shilpika familiar with Delhi, but she also had many friends in the city. Charu (her LSR friend), helped her in many ways. She introduced her to her friend, Gilles Chuyen, a French choreographer, who was auditioning dancers for a production called "COLOURS". "The audition happened through a one-week-long workshop where I was looking at a dancer's vibration", said Gilles. "I think the first impression I had of her was about her presence through her spine. A sense of vertical connection and aplomb. With her Indian classical training and her sculptural beauty, Shilpika stood rather fast for me…as the 'perfect red'".

Gilles went on to work with Shilpika on several different projects over the years. She also became the heroine of his Bollywood musical, "Bollywood Love Story", which toured internationally. "Her charisma, playfulness and ability to emote through her body and face made her shine on stage and created a very special flavour for our show". Besides working with Gilles, Shilpika also decided to learn Mix Martial Arts (MMA), which Charu told her about. "I never looked at them as Martial Arts, but as body movement", said Shilpika, explaining why she decided to learn the hybrid combat sports.

By 2007, Shilpika realised that she liked "playing with my body, exploring what her elbow, knees, shoulders can do". She said she did her first piece with her Martial Arts mentor, Rashid Ansari, who included her in his show. However, a freak accident during this phase left her seriously injured. She was bedridden for three months. Rashid*ji* gifted her a book on monologues for women during this time. She started working with her voice, sound, and text. She performed her second piece at Karmic Research Centre (KRC), founded by Dilip Shankar, for people to work on themselves through creative expression. In 2009, Shilpika participated in the Delhi International Arts Festival. "People were noticing me". Pratibha Prahlad and Arshiya Sethi got in touch with her, and asked her to create a solo piece. Shilpika performed a twenty-minute solo-act. "My first go-to is always Nature", she said. The piece she created was called "Longing–A River's Longing to Meet the Sea", which she performed at the Delhi International Arts Festival as her first original composition.

Her performance was increasingly being noticed by several senior theatre artists. Anuradha Kapur, the then NSD Director, also wanted to meet her as she had heard about her. However, during this phase, Shilpika was being financially supported by her parents. Most of what she was earning, Shilpika continued spending on learning different theatre-dance forms to help her evolve as an artist. Soon, she started receiving choreography project offers from the National School of Drama (NSD). Anuradha Kapur also invited Shilpika to teach at NSD. She continues to be a visiting faculty at NSD. She focuses on Movement work to open minds and immerse in discoveries of and through the body. She did not follow a particular form in her personal style, and that is what she taught her students. Her topics like "discovering and figuring out the inner self and creating your own movement" focus on allowing movement to emerge naturally. Her work with the five elements gives exercises that allow compositions and choreographies to emerge through embodied processes.

FULL BLOOM

(Present)

In 2010, Shilpika took up the Gati Summer Dance Residency (GSDR) to create her own piece. However, she said this was a difficult period for her. "I created my piece with a lot of conflict with the organisation. Everyone was grouping against me when I performed that piece". A renowned dance critic wrote an adverse review in The Hindu on Shilpika's piece. Shilpika said it was a shattering experience for her. However, a week after her performance, a woman called her and asked her if Shilpika could teach her dance. She'd read the Hindu review, and believed that since the older critic had not liked her new approach, she must be doing something right! The woman became her first private student. By this time, Shilpika was also teaching dance part-time at Bluebells School. She was earning enough to afford an independent house. She shifted out of her brother's house and started living in Kalkaji by herself. Here, she started teaching dance to a few students privately. She also changed schools and joined Fr. Agnel School as a regular teacher, but left the school in 2011.

Reconnecting with her Land through Art

She went back to Assam in 2012, but kept travelling to other parts of the country on different interesting choreography and dance projects and as an educator. The journey back to Assam for a creative project became a shift to Assam. It was during this time that she conceptualised her multi-media project called "Katha-Yatra". The aim of this ongoing large-scale project is "a research-based understanding of Brahmaputra, which traverses through the floodplains of Assam. The impressions and understandings of art, culture, identity, development, and the hopes and aspirations of the people inhabiting the banks of the Brahmaputra are intended to be encapsulated in the project, which is part documentation and part re-imagination of the cultural identity and environmental landscape of the river".

The inspiration behind this idea was the result of conversations with one of Shilpika's Pune-based environmentalist friends, Neeraj Vagholikar. The project needed a starting point, and Shilpika decided to initiate it from Majuli island, which she'd visited as a young girl when her dad was posted there. "I premiered my piece on Majuli in 2014 at Sri Ram Centre in Delhi, Rangashankara in Bangalore and Rabindra Bhawan in

Guwahati. Her unique storytelling was noticed and was much appreciated by aesthetes.

"I had a re-imagination of the familiar as an Assamese woman, but the project created a new relationship with my land", she said. "Suddenly, I was no longer thinking about dance and choreography but also about indigenous knowledge systems, traditional clothes, and instruments. There were thirty folk instruments used in this performance piece, live. I'd formed relationships with instrument-makers and elders in the community". Moreover, this was the first full-length production by her.

Shilpika married for a second time, but again, it did not last. She was in Gurgaon in 2014 for one of her performances, where she met her second husband. He was in the Merchant Navy. Within 7 to 8 months of meeting each other, they registered their marriage. The first few months were good, but soon, she realised that they were incompatible. The support she needed to pursue her art was "not available or possible from him", and so after two years, they separated. "Art is who I am", she said. "I'm happy to be on my own right now. The older I get, the more I feel empowered in my existence".

However, on the work front, things were looking good for her. Shilpika was exploring different mediums to tell the stories of her land. For instance, under the Katha Yatra project, she collaborated with a filmmaker, Kamal Musale, who filmed her as she went about researching for 'Majuli', her impressions of her land. The film was created accidentally, and sparked a dormant and new medium for her. She curated cultural residencies and events, and an artist couple from France and local artists did street plays directed by Shilpika, moving 110 km on a tandem cycle and interacting with the community. This experiment was a huge success.

This experience also contributed to the activities of Shilpika's NGO, Brahmaputra Cultural Foundation (BCF), formed in 2013. It is a space of and for community participation, leadership, well-being, and education through arts and culture. "As a cultural activist, I'm talking about stories at risk. I'm a cultural worker. I attempt to facilitate a way that people respect art and artists, educate youth, unlearn, and help them think of it as a livelihood option. BCF is also working with missing tribes in Majuli".

In 2021, Shilpika was approached by the Guwahati government to curate a museum for folk-musical instruments and display them. "We displayed 61 instruments and 151 other such instruments have been identified and ready. We're waiting for the funds so that I can ask artists to make them and display them in the museum called Mahabahu Brahmaputra River Heritage Centre", she said. Shilpika has branched out and continues to do several interesting creative projects under the larger umbrella of her multimedia project, Katha-Yatra, and as part of BCF's initiatives. Recently, Shilpika made her debut Performance Documentary film *Mau—The Spirit Dreams of Cheraw,* which is based on the traditional bamboo dance of Mizoram and the geopolitical history of bamboo in the state. Her film was premiered in August 2023, and is travelling to many national and international festivals for screenings. It is part of a larger series of films on the relationship between humans and non-humans at the backdrop of the climate crisis and culture in Northeast India.

She's passionate about how art should be taught and learnt, and is part of the pedagogical design of a few Performing Art Universities in India. Learning forms a big part of her foundation's (BCF) activity. "Art and its practices have to be taught in an integrated way and also so that people see it as a means of livelihood", she said. "It is multidisciplinary. My relationship with my land expanded me as an artist. It's not only about dance or performance now, but my gaze as a multitudinous artist".

Gagandeep Singh, who knows Shilpika from her Delhi days and has been working with her for the past couple of years, described her aptly with these lines:

> The gift that Shilpika brings on board as a human being and as an artist is her care for people, and valuing their talent and uniqueness. She has gained this quality through her own journey of struggles and triumphs as an

artist. She brings a lot of poise, grace and dignity to all her interactions and creative pursuits, even as a manager at work. She wears multiple hats as an artist, director, actor, dancer, and filmmaker, and does full justice to each of these roles by offering all her commitment and passion.

11

Sweta Jha

Madhubani Artist

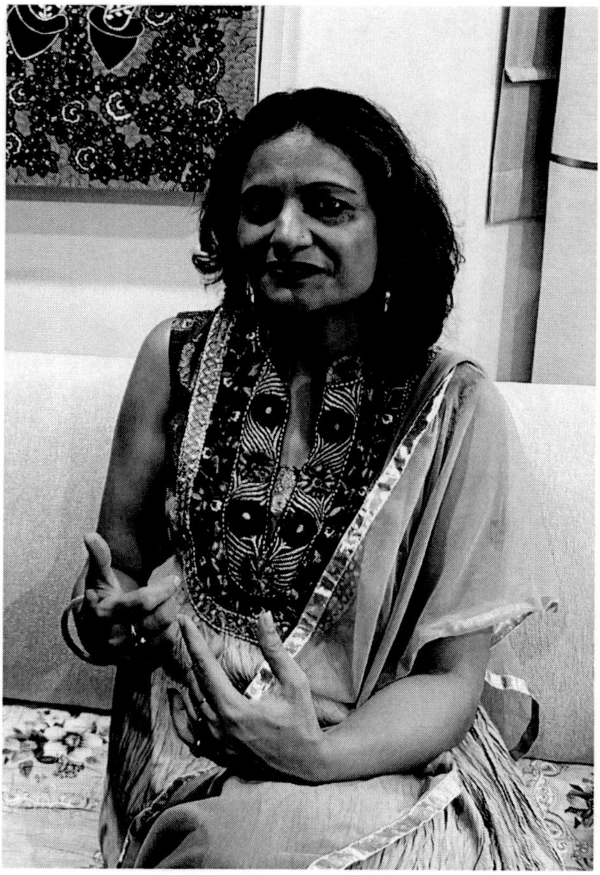

Figure 11

"The fine lines of my works have been pulled from the deep and long tradition of the Mithila/Madhubani art form, and then married to modern metaphors under delicate ministering."

—Sweta Jha

Internationally acclaimed for her *Madhubani/Mithila* (Indian Folk Art) paintings, SWETA JHA (b. 1979) is based in Singapore. Passionate about her work, Sweta uses bright colours, on various objects and art mediums such as canvas, hand-made paper, handicrafts, fabric, personal accessories, wall murals, and more. She has held many art exhibitions, symposiums and workshops in Singapore and abroad. She is also the founder and director of Ttitli Iterations Pte. Ltd. and oversees the activities of her art agency with the help of her husband, Deepak Jha, who is also from Jharkhand and was the first to recognise her talent and encourage her to pursue it. Apart from selling and promoting her paintings, Sweta conducts workshops, trainings and facilitates international art exhibitions related to Madhubani art. She's an International Art Curator as well, and the President of International Action Art, Singapore chapter. Her work has been widely recognised and appreciated in the corporate sector and the grassroots-level community events organised by government agencies. Sweta's paintings have been exhibited widely in art galleries and private collections of art collectors in Singapore, USA, UK, Europe, Korea, Australia, Russia, UAE, Japan and India.

She has been internationally recognized for her exceptional work as a *Madhubani* artist, winning several prestigious awards like Club for UNESCO Awards & Honours (Rome, November 2015), Special Category Gold Medal by Kharamana Art Association, Baghdad (November 2015), Special Award at Moscow Art Symposium by ZERVAS Art Organisation (July 2016), International Award for Talent and Professionals, Madrid, Spain (2017), Metropolitan Empire Prize New York, USA (2017), Craftswoman of the Year Award at International Crafts Awards, India (2018), Dr. Tan Tsze Chor Award,

Singapore (2018), Gandhi Peace Award (2nd October 2020) from The Authors Club Worldwide, and several others.

STAR BUD

(Childhood)

Sweta was born in a traditional middle-class Mithila family in Ranchi, Jharkhand. Her (late) mother, Kamal Jha, was a homemaker, and her (late) father, Suresh Jha, worked at the post office. Sweta said she opened her eyes to see the abundance of nature around her, which got accentuated by *Madhubani* art—a natural part of her culture and immediate environment. "I naturally and unconsciously picked it up at a very early age". Being the youngest of five siblings (four sisters and one brother), she was indulged by her three older sisters: Bina, Kiran, and Rajni. Sweta said they took care of her every little wish. She recalled an incident when she was barely five and had a bad fall and hurt her nose. It was her sisters who took turns taking care of her (apart from managing their own studies and other household chores) and nursed her back to health. Her parents were simple people, and while her mom was strict and kept a check on the children, her dad had a jolly nature and indulged the girls. "He was always on our side", she said. There were no helpers in the house, so her mother and sisters would manage all the housework, while Sweta, being the youngest, was always exempted from it.

In studies, she was an average performer and disliked going to school, especially during the rainy season. She said she often skipped Chemistry and Math tests, but enjoyed Hindi. It was an all-girls school, and Sweta said that while she wasn't keen on studies, she enjoyed being with her four close friends. They were a mischievous lot and often pulled pranks on each other. She narrated how she and two other friends once hatched a plot to steal sweets from another friend's tiffin box whose father had a sweet shop. This friend, Roma, would bring sweets daily in her tiffin box but refuse to share with them, so the other three girls decided to distract her somehow and steal it from her tiffin. Every day during the break, one of them would ask Roma to accompany them to the washroom while the other two would steal the sweets from Roma's box. This continued for three–four years, and it was only when the girls were in class ten that the case of the "missing sweets" was fully revealed to Roma.

Dedication to her Craft

Sweta shared that her Sanskrit and Hindi teachers loved her as she was quite good at reciting *shlokas*. She said reading out *shlokas* was easy for her, as she used to recite the same in her house as well. Sweta was also the class monitor in classes nine and ten. She said that while she wasn't very studious, she loved art. She started painting when she was barely five. However, she didn't know that what she was painting was actually *Madhubani* art. She was first attracted to it when she saw her Nani and Mami painting nature, birds, and figurines on the floor in their village house.

"One of my first paintings was a *Ganesha*, but I didn't know it was *Madhubani*", Sweta revealed. Her parents noticed her talent and encouraged her. Her father would often buy or procure the painting materials, and her mother put her in touch with her Mami so she could learn the art. By the time Sweta was in class ten, she was already quite good, and her elder sister put her in a formal art school to help her perfect her style. Sweta began spending a lot of time painting, and often got a scolding from her mother for the same. "Girls and women in those times were discouraged to follow the arts field", she said. "My desires and dreams got suppressed...I fulfilled them later when I shifted to Singapore after marriage".

In fact, most of Sweta's close friends got married even before completing their graduation. But Sweta wanted to study further, and her parents, especially her father, were supportive and wanted all their daughters to go for higher studies. Even in her thinking and behaviour, Sweta differed from most of her contemporaries. Tall, slim and with an inherent knack for fashion, she liked to dress up and wore jeans and t-shirts, keeping up with trends. She said her neighbours and some of her friends would taunt her and say that she had a masculine dressing sense. Sweta also loved playing cricket, and blackmailed the boys from her neighbourhood to allow her to play with them or else she would spoil the cricket pitch. "I was a good bowler", she said.

Sweta's older sister, Rajni Thakur, described her as being "*khuddar*" or self-respecting. She said that while her sister was much younger than her, she never liked being taken lightly and would insist that she be treated just like her other older friends while playing. She also mentioned that while all the sisters went for post-graduation and had an artistic bent of mind, it was only Sweta who persevered. "My dad, looking at Soni's (Sweta's nickname) deep interest in painting, would often bring her paper and painting material", she said. "*Mithila* painting is common in Bihar and Jharkhand, but she innovated and brought in some changes and started using attractive and eye-catching colours. It worked", Rajni elaborated. Sweta's childhood friend, Suman Sinha, recalled how Sweta would spend her extra time in school making drawings. "My mom used to make *Mithila* paintings and Soni would ask her endless questions about the drawings. She was passionate and focused about it", Suman said. The same was attested by Manju *Bhabi*, a neighbour Sweta was close to during her childhood. "Sweta loved to decorate things", said Manju*ji*. "She would come home and make small paintings and hang them in her own house, or gift them to others. She also used to decorate the main gate during *Saraswati Puja*".

Sweta graduated from school in 1992, and by then, her desire to learn and practice the Madhubani art grew even more. She said, "My fascination and avid desire to learn more about this enigmatic art continued to grow, and by the time I reached college and university, I was already good at what I was doing".

"It was only after marriage…when I moved to Singapore in 2007, that I seriously began to pursue my thought of taking my gift to the whole world in a more professional and structured way".

RAY FLORET

(Youth)

In 1993, Sweta joined the Ranchi Women's College for her Intermediate in the Arts stream. "I used to love Geography.

My favourite parts were the practical assignments, using the telescope and other equipment for road surveys", said Sweta. "There was a boys' hostel near our college, and they would pass remarks and throw flying kisses whenever we passed by, but being from a conservative family and having a strict older brother kept me away from being mischievous", she added. "While my mother was strict about our studies, dad was cool. I passed intermediate with second division marks and took admission in Ranchi University to do Geography Honours, which I completed in 1997-98".

Sweta went on to do her master's in oceanography in 2001. It was during this time that she developed a deep interest in the subject. In fact, she's a distinction holder in both her honours and master's courses.

Sweta was also quite popular in college due to her open, friendly, and tomboyish ways. She had an equal number of male and female friends. Her college life was busy and full of different activities, but Sweta continued to devote time to practising *Madhubani*. "I was doing mythology-themed *Madhubani*, depicting the Ram-Sita Marriage or Shiva as *Ardhanareshwar*", she said. She recalls:

> My elder sister got married while I was still pursuing my master's. My Mami brought '*Khobar*' paintings (Maithili traditional paintings to bless the newlyweds) from the village. I learnt to make snakes, peacocks, and other nature symbols, and also learnt about their symbolic meanings. Much later, for my own wedding, I made the '*Khobar*' paintings myself on paper, although it is traditionally done on the walls of the room in which the newlyweds spend the first four nights. It is still there with me.

Despite her love and dedication to the art form, it remained a hobby for her. She would give away the paintings as gifts. Friends and family loved it and appreciated her talent, but that was it. Sweta's good college friend, Soni Kerketta, mentions how her friend loved anchoring events in college. "She also loved singing", Soni said. "We never bunked classes. However, her parents were old and her siblings were away so Sweta had to sometimes miss her classes as she was needed at home to run errands. Yet, she was a '*bindaas*' girl. I saw her paintings hung in her house. People didn't pay attention, but she would still paint in her free time". Another of her good friends from college, Binod Karmakar, said he liked Sweta as she was open and friendly. "During cricket matches, Sweta would cheer for me and my team". Binod, too, like Soni, was quick to point out that while Sweta was busy with different things in life, he often found her painting rangoli or creating beautiful birthday cards to gift to her friends.

Sweta's parents and everyone else at home wanted her to pursue an academic profession. In 2005, Sweta was preparing for her NET exams when her elder brother, Rajesh, found a good match for her. She was married the same year. This was a huge turning point for Sweta, not only in her personal journey, but also as an artist. One of the first things she recalls Deepak told her was that he wanted "a friend, and not so much a wife". His words had a calming effect on Sweta, who was otherwise a bit nervous. The couple moved to Chandigarh immediately after their marriage.

FULL BLOOM

(Present)

Positive Changes after Married Life

Her arranged marriage to Deepak Jha, an IT Professional, changed her life in more ways than one. For the next couple of years, Sweta said, she spent her time adjusting to her new life and getting to know her husband. "We were learning new things together and became good friends". However, her love for her art form couldn't be diminished despite the huge change that her marriage brought in her life. "I used to paint in hiding", she said. "One day, Deepak came home early from work and saw me painting". Deepak's response was rather surprising to her. "He encouraged me to paint in my spare time and decorate the house with my paintings". Life was moving at a steady pace for the two newlyweds, when a couple of surprise turns brought a halt to Sweta's goal of becoming a lecturer. During her NET mains, she discovered that she was pregnant, and in 2006, Deepak also received a job offer in Singapore. After their daughter Saima was born, the family shifted to Singapore. Sweta settled down in her new life and busied herself, managing the house and taking care of their infant daughter.

Turning a Hobby into a Profession

It was sometime in 2008, when her daughter was around a year and a half and started going to play school, that Sweta picked up painting again—but this time on hand-made paper—upon the insistence of her husband, Deepak. She even sold two small paintings at Saima's play school. "That was the first time she'd monetised her paintings", said Deepak. He was not only proud of his wife's talent, but was the first one to realise the huge potential her art had in Singapore. Sweta's paintings on hand-made paper became her trademark after she became established as a *Madhubani* artist. Deepak encouraged Sweta to visit art galleries and meet people. "In those days, no one in Singapore knew about *Madhubani* or entertained Indian art", Sweta said. "I used to visit art galleries often, taking Saima along with me in a pram". However, not many people that Sweta spoke to show interest in *Madhubani* art.

Their reaction did not discourage her. On the contrary, she decided to hold a small exhibition at a friend's house. This friend admired her paintings, and readily offered her house to Sweta to showcase her paintings. To Sweta's surprise and delight, eight of her ten paintings sold. Encouraged by the positive response, Sweta did a solo exhibition in the function hall of her own condominium. Soon, word started spreading about her, and people started recognizing her as a professional Madhubani artist.

It was around this time that Deepak decided to take out a loan and buy a house. The family had to briefly split. Sweta returned to India with her infant daughter, while Deepak continued living in Singapore. This change in their living arrangement was necessary as apart from the additional burden of paying off the house loan, Deepak had also joined a new company and needed to settle down in his new job. However, within six months, Sweta was again back in Singapore. In 2009, the couple shifted to their new house in Melville Park, which had a thriving Indian Community. It was here that her art truly flourished. Many women friends appreciated her work. She started exhibiting her work in her own house and other places.

A great opportunity presented itself in the form of a big trade fair in 2012, which also became a turning point in Sweta's artistic journey. The event manager of the trade fair informed Sweta that she could display her artwork in a small stall, which would cost them SGD 2000 for a week. It was a significant amount, but the two took a chance, and Sweta displayed her work. Deepak said that while not many paintings were sold in the week-long event, he observed that people were curious and thronged the small stall, asking questions and showing interest. "I felt happy and was sure the idea would work. I had this inhibition earlier that anything to do with art requires a lot of space and money. But after the trade show, I became enthused and started looking out for a small place to stay visible in the marketplace". Also, upon the suggestion of a close friend, the couple finally decided to formalise the business, and Ttitli Art Gallery, Singapore, came into existence in 2013. Sweta said she kept this name because when she was young, she wanted to fly. Everyone used to say, "*Titli ban ke udti rehti hai*".

They found a small 65-square-foot shop for displaying Sweta's work at the Tanglin Shopping Centre at Orchard Road, a prominent shopping location with great footfall. "Not even four people could sit in that space, but it was a good spot", said Sweta. It was glass-covered, her paintings were visible, and the rental was SGD 1800 per month, which they could manage. "I would paint in my shop, and people would stop by, ask questions and leave". Sweta would often paint in her shop, mostly related to Nature, but her favourites were *Ganesha* and *Buddha* paintings, and continue to be so. Lucy Lo, an art seller, owned a gallery right next to Sweta's shop. Lucy admired Sweta's dedication and loved her artwork. The two soon became friends and often spent time together. They have known each other for over a decade now. Sweta said that Lucy has been like a mother to her from the start. "She has always helped and praised me, and often invited her friends and customers to my shop and made them sit and watch me paint. When we bought our new house, she came to bless us".

Receiving Fame and Accolades

Soon, Sweta's paintings started getting noticed, and she started making money. "I could easily make five or six thousand (Singapore) dollars on a monthly basis after a few months", she revealed. Her high point came when, in 2013-14, Mr. Ong Teng Huat, a big art collector from Singapore, was visiting Tanglin Shopping Centre and noticed her paintings and included her as one of the 10 Master Artists in Singapore (and the only female). He bought 55 of her paintings in three months, which were later exhibited in his art gallery. Sweta earned around SGD 20,000 by selling her paintings to him. Her popularity grew, and other art collectors and institutions started getting in touch and placing orders with her. A large MNC from Australia got in touch and placed an order with her.

Her patrons and buyers include prominent public figures and private collectors of Singapore. She has donated a 6×6 feet painting to the Prime Minister's Office, an artwork titled "*Divyashakti*", depicting urbanization and deforestation in a decade. "I felt like a princess when they put up the painting in the PM's office", said Sweta. UoB founder's daughter, Ms. Wee Wei Ling (and herself the founder of *Tatler Asia*), is an admirer of Madhubani art and has bought several of Sweta's paintings. A well-known doctor from Singapore has been buying paintings from Sweta for over a decade. "People keep me alive through my paintings", she said.

Slowly, Sweta also started getting invitations to events as a curator and met other curators from different parts of the world. In 2015, she attended her first art symposium in Italy. "I did line painting for 11 days. I met several other artists from different parts of the world during my stay there. I also won the Club for UNESCO Awards & Honours at the event. I went to a similar symposium in Moscow and spoke for 15 minutes on art". These international exposures helped her open up as an artist, she said. Sweta has received several prominent international awards over the years, but the one that is extra special to her is The Metropolitan Empire Prize presented by the American Art Museum in 2017. She said that with that award, she realised her childhood dream of visiting America. Also, the recognition as The Craftswoman of the Year in 2018, presented to her by the International Crafts Award in Delhi made her feel proud.

Sweta said that her artistic journey has been that of a loner who has been perpetually struggling to get her work noticed in a country like Singapore, where her traditional folk art had no acceptance when she started, and the challenges were compounded by the very high cost of sustaining a business of this nature in a foreign land. She said she persevered mainly because of the strong support and encouragement of her husband. She's also grateful to have the tremendous support of her father-in-law, Shri Rajendra Jha Mahendra, who not only encouraged her with words, but was the one to procure the art material, especially the special hand-crafted paper for her paintings from Bihar. She also gave credit to her sister-in-law, Jyoti Jha, for her unwavering support and for guiding her in her personal life.

However, the years 2021–2022 were bad for business. Her art gallery could barely survive. Luckily, the shop rentals were reduced by the building owner, there was some government support, and her own savings helped her stay afloat. "I continued to paint during the Covid lockdown and also started teaching an online course on the basics of *Madhubani* to housemaids and Bangladeshi workers. It was a government-aided project". Yet, post-pandemic, the business could never pick up as before, shared Deepak. "Inflation rates are high, rentals are six times what they used to be, so we have to work on a new business model again". Ttitli Art Gallery has moved online now. They still do exhibitions, but most of Sweta's paintings are available through their website. As Deepak said, "Sweta will continue to represent *Madhubani* art. She's gritty and she's brilliant in her work. These traits have seen her through some difficult times and will continue to help her progress as an artist. I'm so proud of her that she continues to live true to her art form".

Sweta clearly expressed her own intention, "I'll continue to paint. It's my life's fuel".

12

Vusat Iqbal Khan

Sufi Singer & Dastango

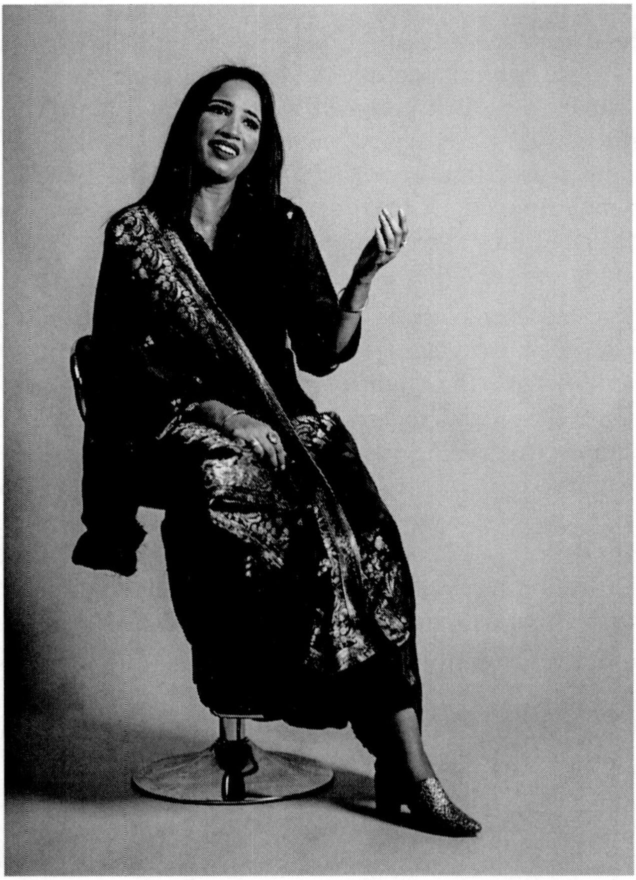

Figure 12

"I have imbibed everything from dad. He is a Sufi. He has lived life as a giver. I have absorbed all that."

—Vusat Iqbal Khan

VUSAT IQBAL KHAN (b. 1985) is a renowned *Sufi* singer, a musical *dastango* of the country, and the torchbearer of the *Dilli Gharana*, the oldest of the *Khayal Gayaki Gharanas* of India. She's carrying forward the 800-year-old legacy of Indian classical music after the passing away of her legendary father, Ustad Iqbal Ahmad Khan. In fact, Vusat's debut song, "*Ishq-e-Haqiqi*", is a heartfelt tribute to her late father. The song is about her story of coping with the loss of her father's passing, and crossed one million views within a couple days of its release. It's also slated to be a part of Naseeruddin Shah's upcoming film. Vusat has brought in a new concept to the organisation, which envisions fusing the artistic treasury of *Dilli Gharana* with Western music instrumentation. Apart from her own compositions, Vusat also sings the rare and soulful compositions of Hazrat Ameer Khusro, the founder of the *Dilli Gharana*.

Vusat has been recognised as a pioneer of musical *dastangoi*, a new style of storytelling in Urdu. She has expertly blended the modern with the traditional flair of the compositions by including the rich repertoire of *Dilli Gharana* in her productions. According to Oxbridge India, some of her well-known and recognised artistic creations are "*Rudaad-e-Shireen*", oriented towards women empowerment (2015), *Dastan-e-Khusro* (2017), and *Ghalib, Begam Umrao ki Nazar Se* (2018). The last has been telecast multiple times on Doordarshan Urdu for its pure musical content and high production quality.

Vusat dons multiple hats with ease. She is also the General Secretary and Treasurer of Sursagar Society of *Delhi Gharana*, founded in 1940. Under her able organising skills, the society organises a variety of cultural events such as the Annual Ustad Chand Khan Festival, Indian Classical Music Festivals, *Sufi* Festivals, *Ghazal* evenings, etc. As a *Sufi* singer and *Dastango*, she has performed on various national and international platforms like the Urdu Heritage Festival, organised by the Delhi Govt.,

World Sufi Festival, Kashmir, Raagmala Foundation, Canada, Alka Jalan Foundation, Kolkata, Shriram Bharatiya Kala Kendra Festival, Delhi, Vishwarang Festival, Tagore University, Dilli Durbar, Delhi, IIM Ahmedabad Theatre Festival, Phool Waalon ki Sair, Government of NCT of Delhi, Delhi International Arts Festival, Prasiddha Foundation Jashn-e-Bahara, organised by DD, Ministry of Information & Broadcasting at Siri Fort Auditorium, Panna Bharat Ram Theatre Festival, Sriram Center, Jashn-e-Khusro, Hyderabad, to name a few.

Vusat's story is that of a devoted daughter who didn't see anything or anyone beyond her father. In a traditional Muslim family where anything to do with music or any other area of performance was restricted only to the men in the house, Vusat was the first woman in her family to break the glass ceiling by not only assisting her father in managing their family-run musical enterprises, but by also becoming the first woman from the renowned musical family to take to stage herself as a *Sufi* singer and carry forward her father's (and the *Gharana's*) legacy.

STAR BUD

(Childhood)

The eldest among four siblings (three sisters and one brother: Aaliya Iqbal, Saad Iqbal & Sadia Iqbal), Vusat Iqbal Khan was born in Delhi to the legendary Indian classical vocalist, Ustad Iqbal Ahmed Khan, and Zohra Khan, in a joint family. Her father was also the Khalifa of the oldest *Khayal Gharana* (also called the *Dilli Gharana*), and thus, music and performance were a natural part of Vusat's growing-up years. She was always surrounded by a musical atmosphere, where renowned artists and music lovers would gather almost daily. "*Mujhe mausiki ka mahaul mila*", said Vusat. Her two-hundred-year-old ancestral house in old Delhi (Mosiqui Manzil) was the venue for well-known regular classical concerts and *Qawwali* nights, and eminent classical singers and musicians of her father's time would gather at the house for musical evenings. A young Vusat absorbed the beautiful sounds of music without realising it. She said she has always been an obedient child and a music lover who was in awe of her father's talent. She never received a formal education in music, but throughout her childhood and adult life, she would hang around her father (or *Abbiji* as she called him) while he practised music or taught his disciples. However, Vusat was a gifted singer, and was often chosen by her teachers to sing and perform in school.

Vusat, together with her siblings and cousins, would also organise in-house music festivals and get their parents and neighbours to watch their performances. "My cousins would play the *tabla*, some would sing. We would organise *mehfils* and get the adults to see our performances", she said.

Vusat did her schooling at a convent school in Delhi. Her parents went against the rest of the family to send all their children to a convent school. Her mother, Zohra Khan, was the first female graduate in the family and completely supported her husband's decision to ensure quality education for their children. Vusat's *Nanaji*, Ustad Hilal Ahmed Khan, was himself a professor in Jamia-Milia-Islamia, and her father was not only her grandfather's favourite student, but also lived with them. The two were so close to each other that often, outsiders mistook their relationship as filial.

Vusat was good at studies, but she was more enthusiastic about co-curricular activities like singing, art, and NCC.

"My childhood was normal", she said. "I was an introvert, and children would often bully me. I was more involved in in-house activities with my cousins than with my school friends". She was quite emotional, and everyone around her would often tell her that. She said she had no interest in household chores, and always knew she had to do something in her life. "We all would play cricket in the *Haveli*", she said. Vusat's mother, Zohra*ji*, said her daughter was a "sharp" girl but also quite "sensitive". She also revealed that her oldest child listened to her. However, she was deeply attached to her father from a young age. "If her father got hurt, Vusat would start crying", she said. Vusat's parents gave her and her sisters the freedom to make choices about their lifestyle. They were allowed to wear clothes of their own choosing despite their traditional background. As a matter of fact, whenever her father visited the US for shows every two to three months, he would pick up skirts for his daughters. "Dad would always stand by us", Vusat said.

Aanchal Gupta, Vusat's childhood friend, reminisced about the good old days she spent in the company of her artist friend. "We went to the same school and were best friends", she said. "Everyone in her family knew my name". She recalled how once Vusat refused to cut her birthday cake just because Aanchal couldn't be there at her birthday party. It was only after Aanchal went to the party accompanied by her mother and sister that Vusat went ahead with her birthday celebrations. "Her family is blessed and Vusat is lucky to be born in that family", Aanchal said. "In their house, the *Geeta* and the *Quran* were always placed together".

She went on to narrate how once in class, after a cricket match in which India had lost to Pakistan, a classmate teased Vusat that she must be happy because Pakistan had won. Vusat was so hurt that she immediately started crying, and told the girl she was an Indian and proud to be one. She also mentioned that teachers loved Vusat because she was an obedient child and was great at music and other extracurricular activities. "I always wanted Vusat to be on stage. She was happy supporting her father...but I knew sometime or the other she would also be in front of the stage". Vusat herself acknowledges that her school teachers loved her, especially her music teacher. "I was the drummer in my school band, but I was so short that I would be hidden behind the drums while playing", she recalled.

RAY FLORET

(Youth)

After passing out from school in 2003, Vusat joined IP College for Women on her father's recommendation to pursue her B.A. (honours) in History, a subject she disliked in the beginning. She was interested in studying Political Science in college, but there were no seats available for the course. Vusat said she was disinterested in her studies, and would often find excuses to bunk her classes. “I rarely attended my classes and would often busy myself with activities outside the class”. Despite her disinterest in studies, she managed to do well during her graduation. In fact, she said she enjoyed college more than school. “I became bold and confident in college”.

She attributes this change in her personality to her joining the college music society. She started taking up responsibilities and played an active part as a member of the music society. Later, she also became the president of the music society, and organised music festivals and other prominent cultural events in the college. It was in college that she also started singing. “I used to sing for fun”. She became extremely popular due to her singing and outgoing nature. Her school friend, Aanchal (who joined a different college), recalled how her younger cousin, who was also in IP College for Women, was completely in awe of her senior. “Vusat’s personality had taken a turn for the better”, Aanchal said. One of Vusat’s college friends, Akshita Mudgal, reminisced about their college life and how Vusat would always be late for lectures but ultimately did well in all the subjects. “She was shy and timid in the beginning, but she evolved”, said Akshita. “I always knew she would do something big”.

An Unconventional Trigger

It was during this time that an incident impacted Vusat deeply, and cemented her resolve to do something in her life, and not fritter it away aimlessly. She was around nineteen when her father sent her to one of his friends, a renowned media personality, to seek his guidance as Vusat was interested in the Media industry. “I told the gentleman I’m interested in media and sought his guidance”. However, instead of encouraging her, the person told her to forget about media and become a teacher instead. “He killed my ambition”, she said. Vusat went back home dejected and cried her heart out. Her father felt bad and consoled her, asking her to forget about what his friend had told her. Vusat worked hard on herself and, in 2006, after completing her graduation, joined a post-graduation course in advertising and marketing with a reputed agency, Exchange for

Media Group. It was here that she also met her future husband, Imran Khan.

Immediately after the completion of her PG course, she was invited to join the global advertising firm, McCann Erickson, and that was the start of her professional journey in the advertising world. Many years later, Vusat met the same gentleman (her father's friend from the Media industry) again at one of her father's musical events, which she'd not only organised but had also performed at as a *Dastango*. By then, Vusat was already well-known on her own account. The gentleman not only praised her for her accomplishments, but also introduced her to his friends as someone talented whom he was proud to know. She said she'd exchanged a secret look of satisfaction with her father that day. "The pride I saw in my dad's eyes was all worth it", she said.

FULL BLOOM

(Present)

Vusat joined the global advertising agency, McCann Erickson, in 2008. She worked with them for a year before she got another break in the Department of Information Technology (Delhi Government) as a Media Consultant. She said she loved her work there even though it involved odd hours. What she enjoyed most was the sense of freedom. She created an anthem as part of her role as a media consultant, which was much appreciated by everyone.

A Fairytale Love Story

Simultaneously, Vusat also started helping her father with organising and managing his events. Another landmark event in her personal life happened around the same time. Vusat got married to her longtime friend Imran Khan in 2010. Their beautiful real-life love story almost seems like it's lifted from a Bollywood romance movie. The two had met while pursuing their post-graduation in advertising and marketing from Exchange for Media Group in 2006. While Vusat considered Imran a good friend, Imran's feelings for her were different from the very moment he set eyes on her. "*Dekhte hi kuch ho gaya tha*", he said. The first time he saw her, she was singing a song at the informal introduction party of the new batch, and he fell for her instantly. Imran proposed to her within the first week meeting, but Vusat rejected him, saying she was there to pursue a professional course.

However, they still became good friends. Imran said everyone in her family came to know of him as Vusat's friend. He started frequenting her house on special occasions and festivals. Imran said everything about Vusat was not only new, but also different to his own background. He belonged to Kanpur, and his father was in a government job. Vusat's family, on the other hand, was into arts and music and with a rich culture. This exposure to music was something he started liking and enjoying, and he got involved in helping out Vusat in planning events too. In 2008, the two organised a musical event, "Sur Sandhya", in Kamani Auditorium, where Shubha Mudgal performed to a packed house. The event was a huge success, he said.

Their friendship bloomed with time. Imran would drop Vusat to work when they both started working, and spent most of his free time with her and their common group of friends. Slowly, he also became close to her family, and once, when Zohra*ji* commented that no one would marry her daughter because of her tomboyish ways—finding the perfect opportunity—Imran told her that he would marry her. By then, Vusat had also come to see him as a close friend and confidant and had fallen in love with him.

The two got engaged in 2009 with the blessings of both families, and were married in 2010. Praising his wife, he said, "From the start, Vusat has been fun-loving, and takes up challenges head-on. I'm calculative. So, she plans, but I execute. Our partnership works well". From the first event, "Sur Sandhya", which they did together with a footfall of 700 to 800 people in 2008, to the extremely popular annual musical event "Dilli Durbar", which saw a footfall of 30,000 people in 2019 (and 1 lakh in 2023), it has been an exhilarating experience for the couple. "While Vusat handles the PR and communication-related aspects and the project proposals, I understand the ground-level work and banking better, so I take care of that part", he said, explaining how they divide the work between themselves.

Finding her Own Tune

After their marriage, the two increasingly became involved in helping her father with managing his musical enterprises, and that is when Vusat decided to quit her job and carry forward the legacy of the *Gharana* with her father and husband. Vusat even started hosting her father's events, and the audience loved it. Her family realised she was excellent on stage and encouraged her further. But it was only in 2015 that her journey as an artist started, when she first learnt about *Dastangoi*. And yet, while she liked the form, she didn't enjoy the traditional style of *Dastangoi* much.

One evening, while she was sitting with her *Abbiji* while he was imparting a lesson to his students, it suddenly occurred to Vusat that it would be great to develop a story around Amir Khusrau (the founder of *Dilli Gharana*) and put it to music. The idea had not been tried yet, and she mentioned the same to her dad, who loved the suggestion and gave her his consent to work on it. There was no stopping Vusat after that. She combined storytelling with music and brought Amir Khusrau's compositions alive.

She became the first female musical *dastango,* and created her first production, "*Rudaad-e-Shireen*", a tale of a woman and her life's journey to find her identity. Her unique concept and effort bore fruit, and the composition was loved by art connoisseurs and music lovers alike, performed to packed houses several times within the first few months of its release. After the success of her first production, Vusat went on to develop several other such interesting projects which had never been tried before in traditional *Dastangoi,* and presented them to the audience with a fresh take on the classical high-art form with a focus on women-oriented stories. A family friend, Ms. S. Radha Chauhan, a prominent bureaucrat who has known Vusat since she was a young professional, said:

> Vusat is a brilliant, passionate, and sensitive individual who has traversed a very hard and challenging path. And I have seen her on this journey for a little less than two decades now. At times, I thought she could have chosen an easier way to lead her life...she had a promising career and with her vibrant personality, she could have easily charted a much more predictable and less challenging career for herself, but most admirably, she didn't do so. She was steadfast in her resolve to pursue what she had inherited through generations of pure pursuit of art and music.

Her journey had well begun. But not many knew at that time—except perhaps her immediate family—was as a highly sensitive individual, Vusat was also tackling emotional challenges in her life as she flourished as an artist. Dr. K Khurana, Vusat's mentor, therapist, and friend, said she came to him with existential issues in 2015. She was looking for answers to "life's challenges", he said. As the daughter of a famous father, Vusat was constantly under scrutiny by others around her and under self-imposed pressure from the time she came into the limelight. "Undue comparison is something the second generation suffers", said Dr. Khurana. Vusat overcame her emotional challenges after she came in touch with Dr. Khurana. She continued to remain in touch with him even after she had bloomed personally and professionally. He said, "she's been someone carrying the mirror to help her reach her goals".

Vusat's good friend, Anika Singh, whom she met in 2018 through common interests and work, and instantly formed a connection with, said that what she finds amazing about her friend is that she reflects on everything. Whatever she does, she does it from the heart. Both friends treat each other as "soul sisters". The two have collaborated on several unique artistic projects in the social space, garnering critical praise and admiration for their work.

A Devastating Loss

Things changed drastically for Vusat when her beloved father passed away suddenly in December 2020. She broke down completely, and her life came to a standstill. "Her entire existence was devoted to her father and the two-hundred-year-old *Dilli Gharana,* and when he passed away suddenly, she felt her life had lost its purpose", said Anika. No one knew how to get through to her. "She had switched off from the world and went into severe depression", said Anika. All her other friends, her family, and especially her husband and mother, became worried and expressed the same concern. Vusat refused to interact with anyone and shut herself in her room for months. All she did was cry relentlessly. It took the combined effort of her family, close friends, therapist, and most importantly, her spiritual *guru*, Hazrat Riazuddin Chishti in Ajmer Sharif Dargah, to bring her out of her depression and start leading a normal life again.

Vusat claims that her greatest moment in life was meeting Hazrat*ji* in Ajmer. She was introduced to him by a good friend. That first meeting became a turning point in her life. "She's amazing as an artist because she's a generational talent, and is into her art both by birth and by choice as well", said Hazrat*ji*. He said that the change in her outlook towards life and her career was brought about through *Sufi* teachings. "During her depression, she was going towards fundamental Islam, and I attracted her towards liberal *Sufi* thought and brought forth her true self. She's a real *Sufi* traveller with a deeply loving nature, a very strong faith, and now she has achieved great mental strength and she's the best artist in my eyes", Hazrat*ji* further revealed.

Rebirth

This was also a new turn in her life. Vusat disclosed that there was a point in time after her father's demise when she wanted to become a *nastik*. "I had died with my dad", she said. "This is a rebirth. When I met Hazrat*ji*, I felt peaceful. He said to me, dad is within me. And he asked me, who will run the tradition? Then he told me to start singing and carry forward the baton I'd been given". It was only after this beautiful encounter with her spiritual guru that Vusat decided to compose *Ishq-e Haqiqi*. "I wrote it for my father", she said. After completing the musical tribute, she showed it to Hazrat*ji*. He told her, "You're born to love. You've written the song and now sing it". Vusat disclosed, "I got a call from a music producer, Aditya Gulati, who wanted to work with me. Aditya would carry my father's picture and I would get emotional while filming the song".

Her song became an instant hit with music lovers, and marked the beginning of her special journey as a *Sufi* singer. "I'm a practising *Sufi* now and I only sing love. The only way to *Sufism* is to spread love", Vusat said. "I go to Ajmer once or twice a month with my husband and mother. All my small and big wishes have been fulfilled. I feel peaceful. Papa's tradition has to be carried forward and I'll continue that", she said. "Also, my son, Aalif Iqbal Khan is a big strength in my life, as he understands me the most and is the best thing that has happened to me".

From a shy and timid girl who sang for fun in college, to a renowned *Sufi* singer who is also determined to carry forward the legacy of her father, Ustad Iqbal Ahmed Khan (and the *Dilli Gharana*), Vusat has evolved into a beautiful artist, writing, and singing songs of hope, joy, and peace. As her mentor and therapist, Dr. Khurana puts it, "When she smiles with her eyes wide open, that's who she is, a flower that blooms".

Bibliography

Admin. "*Ishq-e-Haqiqi* 09 April 2022 – *The Oxford and Cambridge Society of India*." The Oxford and Cambridge Society of India, April 11, 2022. http://www.oxbridgeindia.com/event/past-event/ishq-e-haqiqi-09-april-2022/.

Art Safe Gallery. "Sweta Jha | *ArtSafe Gallery* | Singapore," n.d. https://www.artsafesg.com/sweta-jha.

Brahmaputra Cultural Foundation. "About -," June 18, 2023. https://bcf-india.org/.

Khurana, Chanpreet. "*Choiti Ghosh: The Puppeteer Who's Injecting Magic into Everyday Objects*." Scroll.In, May 10, 2016. https://scroll.in/article/807790/choiti-ghosh-the-puppeteer-whos-injecting-magic-into-everyday-objects.

Mahmood, Nida. "*About Us* | Nida Mahmood | Queen of Kitsch," n.d. https://www.nidamahmood.com/about.html. https://www.diginow.co.uk/. "Pelva Naik | Darbar," n.d. https://www.darbar.org/artist/Pelva%20Naik.

MumbaiTheatreGuide.com. "*Interview with Choiti Ghosh Interview*: www.MumbaiTheatreGuide.Com," n.d. https://www.mumbaitheatreguide.com/dramas/interviews/choiti-ghosh-interview.asp.

Mysite. "About the Author | *Dragons & Rainbows*," n.d. https://www.dragonsandrainbows.com/about-the-author-hina-siddiqui.

Nevatia, Shreevatsa. "*Writing up a Storm | Cinema*." India Today, June 14, 2019. https://www.indiatoday.in/magazine/leisure/story/20190624-writing-up-a-storm-cinema-1547961-2019-06-14.

Pragya Jain. "About — Pragya Jain," n.d. https://www.pragyajain.com/new-page.

Reporter, Staff. "Musical Tribute to Help Cope with Loss, Fill Void." The Hindu, March 24, 2022. https://www.thehindu.com/news/cities/Delhi/musical-tribute-to-help-cope-with-loss-fill-void/article65255775.ece.

Sinha, Komal. "Kanika Dhillon Talks About The Impact Of The Manmarziyaan Controversy." Talepost, May 29, 2020. https://

talepost.com/kanika-dhillon-talks-about-the-impact-of-the-manmarziyaan-controversy/.

www.meetkalakar.com. "Book Arushi Mudgal for Event | Request Arushi Mudgal for Performance | Learn Hindustani Classical Vocal, Kathak, Tabla, Light Vocal, Flute, Harmonium, Sitar, Modern Dance Forms, Bharatnatyam," n.d. https://meetkalakar.com/Artist/2511-Arushi-Mudgal.

www.kaurmanjot.com. "About | Www.Kaurmanjot.Com," n.d. https://www.kaurmanjot.com/bio.

Questionnaire

Online Interview

Basic Profile

Name

Age

Marital Status

Family

Artist's Profession

Place of Birth/Parental Home

Current Place of Residence

Childhood

What were you like as a child?

What are your first memories of childhood?

Are you the only child or do you have siblings?

A bit about your parents. Their nature, professions and your relationship with them in your childhood.

Your relationship with your siblings.

Things you enjoyed doing. School life including your interest areas. Best friends. Any particular person/friend who influenced you during your childhood.

Any significant event from that period which impacted you.

What were your aspirations/ambitions as a child?

Names and coordinates of your childhood friends, teachers or other people whom you were close to.

Any special memory of your childhood you still carry with yourself.

Youth

What was College life like?

Did you pursue your interest area from the start?

When did you realise you wanted to be an artist?

How did you steer towards the journey of becoming an artist?

Who were your close confidants/friends in this period of your life? A couple of names (with their coordinates).

Challenges you faced during this time. And how did you manage it.

Any loss/failure/hardships that you would like to talk about from this period and how it shaped your thinking.

People in your professional journey who helped you and how.

A new skill or learning that helped you sharpen your art.

When and what was the first breakthrough in your artistic journey?

How did you take it?

What was the response/reaction of your family and friends after you achieved success for the first time in your field? The person you reached out to after your first win...

Any other significant event or personal/professional interaction from this period you would like to mention.

Present

Describe your adult self.

What are some of the prominent qualities that have kept you in good stead and helped you grow?

What is it that you enjoy most as an established artist?

What do you do to enrich yourself as an artist?

What's your routine like when you're home?

Any major challenge(s) you face as an artist and as a woman after becoming established in your field?

What is it that helps you feel grounded as an artist and as a person?

What's the best moment and the best compliment that you received in recent times?

Any cause or activity apart from your professional work you're passionate about and involved with to make this world a better place?

Any significant event/interaction that left an indelible mark on you?

Your future plans and goals?

NOTE:

- A short note mentioning the artist's major works/ achievements will go with high res pics of the artist. Artist Profile and pics needed for the same.
- Please share important interviews, links, articles et al.
- Relevant pics, milestones, (first exhibition, performance, artwork, award et al) and also quotes/endorsements by other artists will be required and included at relevant places in the book.

In Person Interview (and Photo Shoot)

1. How does your routine work-day look like?
2. Which is the best part of the day?
3. Do you work alone or you have your team working alongside you?
4. Do you allow your friends and family to take a look at your unfinished work?
5. Which is the best stage of your artistic endeavor? The beginning, middle or the end?

Interview Questions for the Artists' Contacts

Parents/Teachers

1. How was she (the artist) as a child/youth?
2. Mention a few traits/attributes you admire in her.
3. Do share an incident that you can recall showing her dedication and passion for her art practice from her younger days.
4. Anything else you wish to share is welcome.

Friends/Associates

1. How did you meet?
2. What was it that struck you about the artist as a person?
3. Mention a few attributes/traits that you think stood her in good stead in her artistic as well as personal growth.
4. Please share an incident(s) showing the artist's lighter/fun side or passion for life in her younger days or even now.
5. Anything else you wish to share is welcome.

About the Author

Sujata Parashar, a prolific author, gained recognition with her debut novel *In Pursuit of Infidelity* in 2009, followed by successful works like *In Pursuit of Ecstasy* and *In Pursuit of a Lesser Offence*. Her socio-political thriller *The Temple Bar Woman* earned the A3F Foundation Best Fiction award in 2021.

Beyond fiction, Sujata co-wrote *The Sundesh Story* for Dabur India's CSR in 2019 and released *In Pursuit of Mi Amor* in 2021, dedicated to the Hemophilia community. Her hand guide on single parenting *Going Solo: Raising Happy Kids* won the PVLF Excellence Award in 2021.

A social activist, trainer and talk therapist, Sujata was a founding member of Empowering Minds and contributed to the Parents Empowering Parents (PEP) program. Her talk-therapy platform The Talk–it–Out–Express (TiOE), launched in 2019, promotes emotional health. She also serves as Vice President of WICCI's Arts Leadership Council (Delhi). She has been the recipient of prestigious awards such as 100 Women Faces in 2018, Karmaveer Chakra Award in 2016 and 2019, Women Achiever of 2021 and the PVLF Author Excellence Award in 2022. In 2022, she was recognized as an Iconic Author by Women Economic Forum and received the Progressive Women's Award from Aesthetics International.

Other Works Authored by the Writer:

Novels

- In Pursuit of Infidelity (2009)
- In Pursuit of Ecstasy (2011)
- In Pursuit of a Lesser Offence (2014)
- In Pursuit of Mi Amor (2021)
- The Temple Bar Woman (2018)

Non-Fiction

- The Sundesh Story (2019)
- Going Solo – Raising Happy Kids (2021)

Short Story

- That Woman You See (Alchemy)
- The Curlew (UK): Mountains Don't Preach (Nature Essay)

Poetry

- Poetry Out and Loud (2012)
- Poetry Out and Loud I (2013)
- Poetry Out and Loud II (2014)